AF824767

FOOTE'S CONVEXITY BOOK

Convexity and Value: A DIY Guide to Smart Investing

ABSTRACT

This is a book bout convexity investing, seeking asymmetric returns and doing it yourself

Brian William Foote, CFA

First Edition

Copyright © 2023 by Brian William Foote, CFA

All rights reserved.

No portion of this book may be reproduced in any form without written permission from the publisher or author, except as permitted by U.S. copyright law.

To Monica

TABLE OF CONTENTS

ACKNOWLEDGMENT

Nothing in this book should be construed as investment advice, and references to specific companies and strategies should be considered as general reference and not recommendations. Brian William Foote, CFA is not an accountant, lawyer or tax advisor, either. Trading in stocks and derivatives involves a substantial amount of risk, including total loss of capital.

CHAPTER 1
CONTRARIANS ONLY

Do you have the contrarian mindset, the temperament to be an investor? This is a book about demystifying stock picking. If you believe you are NOT a contrarian and lack the temperament, this book can still assist you in asking the "right questions" to your advisors. The terminology, jargon, lingo, and other seemingly mystical elements, in my mind, merely serve to elevate the perception of what individuals in my industry do, which is essentially buying fractional interests in businesses. And you want to buy good businesses at good prices. That's all it is.

There is a lot written on this topic. In fact, I will recommend multiple books and websites to you. I think that demystifying things for the educated entrepreneur (like you) is one of the best things I can do. I have done this for 25 years; in fact, I started as a professional when I just turned 19 years old, when I got registered as a stockbroker in 1993. To celebrate that 30th anniversary, I want to share tricks that I've picked up over the years. My training as a civil engineer helped me to break seemingly complicated things, like buildings, bridges, dams, roads and even sewerage treatment plans, into easy-to-model abstractions. At the end of the day, the tallest skyscraper is a collection of elements working in unison to combat gravity and other elements—the individual column and bolt can be (and is) modeled and calculated by an engineer using the same basic techniques taught to me as a freshman, my professors before me, and all the way back to when Isaac Newton formalized his laws. The stock market is a LOT less complicated than that.

The stock market is merely a "place" where people trade fractional interests in companies. When I was a kid, that was indeed a place being replaced rapidly by electronic trading. But just like the skyscrapers my engineering school colleagues build, there is still a basic element—the exchange of cash for interest in a business.

Is the stock market a mystical place? NO, decidedly not. I have been scolded by people in my family and friend group not to demystify the stock market because—to them—it's "all black magic." That is PRECISELY what brokers and other practitioners want you to think. I am not attempting to eliminate the position of broker or banker because they do serve a purpose, albeit an informational one—I have benefitted greatly over the years from speaking with extremely knowledgeable individuals who work as stockbrokers and investment bankers working for a commission. On average, though, the brokerage houses would be out of business if they put up a sign saying, "The Stock Market is Not Mystical" and "We do NOT practice black magic here." The work of someone buying a collection of good companies at good prices CAN be done by someone with 1) a contrarian streak, 2) curiosity, 3) command of basic math, 4) shameless plug—a book like this!

My job is to show you that you have the basic ingredients ALREADY IN YOUR HEAD AND EXPERIENCE.

Does it require a ton of expertise?

Yes and No. Again, you need to come to the stock market with the premise, that of a contrarian, that you can identify and buy a piece of a business from someone else (they're faceless) at a fair price. If you've been to a supermarket, a car dealer, or a restaurant, you already have part of this temperament. If you collect baseball cards, comic books, art, whatever, you already have the streak within you. If you have ever bet on a horse race with some degree of knowledge about the horse, the jockey or the trainer, you have the right streak. If you've ever negotiated a price for something—a house, a car, a copy of Iron Man 1, you have been on the right path.

Do you like bargain hunting? Price comparisons for air travel? Maybe you can go on eBay to add something to your collection? You have the right experience on this path.

Do you ever walk into a restaurant and think about how they could run it better? Or walk the aisles in your favorite supermarket and consider why this one is successful, but its predecessor is out of business? Ever walk the mall and see apparel stores thriving while others, once popular, are bankrupt? These are the kinds of investigative questions to consider.

Yes, there is a bunch of jargon, EBITDA this and FED FUNDS that, but what you should be concerned with, what Warren Buffett is generally concerned with, is "am I buying a piece of a good business at a fair price." The ability to judge is already available to most people with a high school education and a bit of a contrarian streak and curiosity. Is the cash coming out of a business more than the cash coming in? Is the management team generating a positive return on all the capital employed in the business? Is the business competitive with others? You'd ask precisely the same question if you were buying a lemonade stand or a paper route. And that sort of stuff is done by preteens, maybe even once by YOU.

Is it charts? NO

I have survived a quarter-century career and have watched investors make 7, 8 and even 10-figure incomes, NEVER looking at charts. My mentor in the business shunned charting. The only rich chartists, he said, were the ones selling chart books. This is, in some circles, a controversial statement, and there is a level of religiosity that some people attribute to charting. Here's a rule—be religious about avoiding religiosity. I do know people who swear by them, but it's extremely difficult—if not impossible to replicate what they are up to. I am here to save you time and to demystify something. Charts add a degree of fake physics and scientific cache to what practitioners are doing. I don't use them, and I don't recommend spending time on them.

Is it like ESPN? Again, NO

Let me explain. You can do extremely well in the stock market without ANY television. In fact, for many, and I'd argue most, people, the television is not a good place to be if you're serious about investing. Television exists to sell you something while entertaining you. CNBC and Bloomberg TV have wonderful—often extremely insightful commentators, great interviews by intelligent journalists and a lot of good news to boot. Do you need any of this to win? Nope. Do you need to scroll through real-time quotes to the bottom of the screen? Not at all. I'm not teaching you anything by saying this, but CNBC and Bloomberg datapoint bingo are not at all necessary for you to develop a good investment program. And worrying about "did they beat or miss analyst estimates" is similarly meaningless over time. View the "analyst consensus" as a collection of salesmen and saleswomen coming to a point estimate about what a company does over a 90-day period. It's fun to watch, but the real job of analyzing a business to buy is figuring out what the business will earn OVER TIME and not just an average of a bunch of point estimates.

So the stock market is not mystical, it's not colorful charts, and it's not a sports channel.

It's mundane. To some, it's pretty boring. It best when it is a game of subtraction, a game of figuring out what to avoid! You come up with a collection of industries you deem "too hard" to figure out. That's trick one. Rule out industries where you are either going to be bored or that you don't have an interest. You're likely left with a pile of companies and industries that DO interest you. We'll discuss this more in later chapters on screening. You want to draw what Buffett calls the "circle of competence." And then, you want to read everything you can about these businesses.

As of this writing, it's the end of 2023. You can go on the internet, and the SEC has made available (by law) the annual and quarterly reports of every publicly traded company in the US, plus foreign issuers who sell stock on our exchanges. Even better, your industries and companies have investor relations websites where you can find the glossy versions of the annual reports and often investor presentation PowerPoints that you can examine. You're basically doing the work I did back in high school, going to the library for the Junior Year English assignment—you're doing it from the comfort of your home. Later, I'll show you short cuts of exactly where you should look within the annual and quarterly reports for the nuggets you'll need to make a basic determination of what you should own.

It is easy to figure out, once you have the right drivers to look for. No one who makes a commission is going to tell you this, but this labor (going to a website, downloading an annual report, reading it, taking notes) is extremely easy. Within those pages, admittedly, can be shenanigans. Consider Enron as the BIG shenanigan company. Later, I'll show you how to avoid these sorts of things (preview—something like Enron couldn't be explained easily, and if you can't write in a sentence what a company does and how they make money, put it on the "too hard" pile)

Remember, this is all about rejection.

Consider the "if then statement" in computer programming—if it is too hard, then cast it away.

Detective work. A lot of what we do as investors can be likened to detective work. The better you are at sniffing out BS, the better you can be as a short seller. The better you are at figuring out what restaurants are growing and what are going out of business, the better you'll be as a restaurant investor. Don't let this be daunting to you. Sometimes, things are blatantly obvious. And, you don't need to have major investigative abilities to figure out if a company is a good or even great investment. You just need better-than-average curiosity.

You bought this book (or better yet, someone bought it for you), so you are already better than average. The best in the business are indeed better than Sherlock Holmes. They are always figuring out the right metric, the crucial key performance indicator others haven't. I've seen many of them come from industries OTHER than Wall Street—they have a good sense of what makes a great investment because they've actually allocated capital away from Wall Street.

Yeah, but what about all the high-level math you'll need?

This is also about basic algebra and probability. Sure, some of my heroes—you'll read about them later, are literally masters of mathematics (actually, they are literally Doctors of Mathematics). Nassim Taleb, Jim Simons, and Ed Thorp are names you SHOULD know. And you should learn to THINK like Professor Taleb if you are going to do this business right.

However, to pick stocks, you do NOT need to possess these maestros' tremendous education.

Can you multiply and divide? Then, all the ratios they discuss on TV: Earnings Per Share, PE (price to earnings), and Return on Equity will be easy. So will Return on Invested Capital and Free Cash Flow.

Can you subtract? Then gross profit, pre-tax profit, and net income will all make sense to you.

Did you pass fractions? Good, then you'll be ok with discounted cash flows.

Can you calculate percentages? And do you know how to do simple interest calculations? We learned this stuff in fourth grade (thanks, Mrs. Harris) and I am sure you know it!

Do you understand the probabilities of a coin toss (fair coin) or a 6-sided die? Then, you will have a good grounding in the handicapping used to figure out stock target values.

A bit of algebra can come in handy, but not stuff like the Pythagorean theorem (which Mr O'Shea taught us, and I got 100 on that test, but I've never seen that in investing!)

How did I get into this business, and why do I love it (and why should you?) —Argumentation. From an early age, I found the debate to be extremely appealing. If you enjoy a good argument, a nonviolent one about politics, religion, philosophy, or favorite teams, you will find investing in the stock market appealing.

The basic mechanism in the stock market is buying a piece of a business from someone else. You can have many figurative and literal derivatives of that. The literal derivatives are my second love, options. But, at its crux, strip everything away, but a share of stock is a share in a business. After everything is left, meaning after all the debt is covered, you're the owner of a slice of that company's profits. You most likely bought it from someone else in the secondary market (the Stock Market). If you bought it from the company, you participated in an initial public offering (IPO). But in either case, you are the owner of that possibly microscopic but nevertheless very real interest in a business.

That's, in my view, cool. And what's even cooler is that if you bought it in the secondary market, you bought it from someone else who deemed it NOT as desirable as the cash you spent on it. You made an argument that until you sell the share, it is MORE desirable than the cash you put to work. That's a central and crucial theme because if you made that decision, you're going to have to come up with supporting arguments to back that up. You worked hard for that cash, and you just—via the magic of electronic trading—fired that cash into the bank account of the seller of that fractional interest in the business. Ask yourself, did that person know more than you? Are they better at assessing the value of the business than you? Is it the cousin of the CEO? Or, are they about to go on vacation and view that cash for the trip superior to the investment? Or, maybe it's a fine business at a great valuation but they've found even better. You'll likely never know who the "other side of the trade" is, but the more you can role play and the more you can come up with reasons WHY you bought, as well as real reasons why the other side might be selling, the better you will be. There will be both qualitative AND quantitative reasons for this. You may make a list of 100 reasons. It's actually very fun and a practice I recommend. Email me at brian@broadwaycap.com and we can discuss.

I love writing expository prose. Back in my senior year of high school, I was introduced to the art of building expository prose. I loved the elegance and simplicity of this, which was designed by our beloved senior AP English teacher, Mr. Fili, to help us ace the AP exam and—in his words—to prepare us to help the young women of the boarding school set write their college essays (this was the early 1990s and it was an all men school). Yes, I got the 5, and yes, I married a young lady from that set, thanks in some part to my writing abilities!

The basics are this. You have a thesis; you state that thesis. You have three supporting arguments, but you ALSO have three conceded points that you deconstruct. Your final paragraph synthesizes all of this.

Can you do the same thing regarding stocks you own? Can you come up with a reason you bought it? Can you have at least three risk factors, qualitative OR quantitative, about why this might not be a good investment for a good business? Can you give counterpoints in support of your thesis (buying the business)? If you cannot, you shouldn't be buying the thing! There are many stocks out there where I am CERTAIN I don't know. So what? You could come up with this kind of argumentation. This is why I said you need a high school education to do this kind of job.

Love argumentation, debate, and "mock trial"

Early in my life, I really took to three things: 1) board games, especially Monopoly, 2) business ideas, like paper routes, lemonade stands, whatever Thurston Howell III did, and 3) argumentation. In high school, I gravitated toward mock trial/moot court and the debate team. People would argue with me for fun, with my own family telling me to "go to law school" in a pejorative way. I wanted to go into the investment world. To many in my family, that was viewed as speculative, as something you had to "have the innate talent to do." My grandfather insisted law school was a good course. All I needed was to read Peter Lynch's "One Up on Wall Street" to completely disabuse me of that notion.

Bet against the crowd. Don't be a follower.

A couple of things were very evident to me from an early age. Bet against the crowd. That was an early lesson I had drilled into my head by my grandmother—don't get with the crowd. I was especially rewarded growing up in a working-class grammar school, where "the crowd" were the kind of kids who mocked academic success and—almost to a boy—believed that wearing football team jackets entitled them to walk onto NFL teams right after high school. I didn't like football; I was more of a Yankee fan, and Monopoly.

I really enjoyed Math, Science, History and Writing. Decades later, I got to incorporate the qualitative and quantitative. I also had a competitive streak, which I think you need to do this.

Here are some things you really DON'T need to level the playing field against the competition.

You don't really need Money. Obviously, that's wrong since you need some money to buy stocks, but what I mean is money with a capital M. Don't believe me? Given that in some years, over 80% of actively managed funds, replete with $100s of millions of investment research budgets, actually UNDERPERFORM the index benchmarks and index funds that devote zero to active research, the point is proven. Any of the major brokerage houses, with armies of analysts, have their picks underperform dart throwing. And, as I've seen in the industry, pedigree from a wealthy family or expensive school is NOT a predictor of success. Do NOT be impressed by any pedigree other than what is called "alpha"—the ability to pick stocks that give excess return (in fact, you don't really need to understand too many Greek letters to be massively successful, I promise!) The lucky sperm club might get people their start in picking stocks, but the wonderful thing about the stock market is that it doesn't care if you come from the Ivy League or the local little league when you pick stocks. You also do NOT need a rich uncle or connections to be successful. Sure, Warren Buffett went to Columbia Business School. Charlie Munger went to Harvard Business School. However, Munger has admitted he never took a course in economics.

The stock market isn't really an Insider game. There are caveats to this, too, since members of Congress can—and do—often trade on information that hasn't reached the general public. Don't do this (though you can look at Congressional trades for idea screening!) Yes, you will get blindsided occasionally by this sort of thing, but for the most part, I have found the stock market to be a fair game where hard work and differential insight CAN be rewarded. The market isn't really stacked against an industrious individual or a smaller fund. Sure, there are cheats—people who actually do trade illegally (or at least unethically) based on an unfair advantage. In my career, that sort of thing has been an exception, not a rule.

I'd even point out that you don't need any expensive research services or any research services other than just reading annual and quarterly reports and listening to company conference calls. While I run my fund with a research budget, it is NOT stratospheric by any means, and I rather enjoy mimicking the early Buffett in this regard. I will point out some wonderful screening and financial data services that don't cost very much, but trust me, you do NOT need to spend more than a few thousand dollars a year to have a great advantage over the unenterprising.

Prove them wrong

Another wonderful thing about the stock market. You can short! This is especially appealing to an argumentative son of a b#tch like me. Shorting has its own set of rules and own set of very pronounced risks. Don't do this at home. Use puts instead. Simple enough. I'll spend a bit of time on this because I view understanding HOW to short as integral to understanding how to buy—you NEED to understand why a stock could be a good short candidate.

For those unfamiliar with this terminology, shorting a stock entails borrowing shares from your brokerage (there is an interest cost), selling them, receiving cash and using that cash (if you're right) to buy back shares at a lower price. To be profitable in a short position, you must be able to "cover" the shares at a price lower than the price at which you sold the borrowed shares (with enough profit to cover the interest you paid to borrow the shares).

So, who are the top three enemies you have in the stock market? 1) Yourself. You can be your own biggest enemy. The moment you buy a stock, you have entered into a world in which your overconfidence will do battle with your self-doubt. You can never be 100% certain, or—by definition, there'd be no reward. 2) Chance. You will have done all the work you could do to be satisfied with making the purchase, but you have made a bet on that work, and the future is uncertain since it is the future. The day before the BP-owned oil well in the Gulf of Mexico blew up back in 2010, I had friends who had bought shares of all the companies involved. And many of them had extremely sound reasons for doing so—that well had a LOT of oil in it, for instance. The problem was that oil uncontrollably leaked into the Gulf and caused billions of dollars of damage.

You will lose sometimes, even if you have all the facts and circumstances roughly right. These are minority interests in companies run by people and subject to uncertainty.

The final enemy is a guy (not a woman, because this level of extreme impulsiveness couldn't be female) Ben Graham called "Mister Market."

Mr. Market

THIS is the guy you're trading against. Picture someone on the other side of your trade who is emotional, often idiotic, impatient. He is basically the reverse of Mr. Spock. Here's a temperament tip—if you can be unemotional, intelligent, and patient and emulate Mr. Spock in the way you approach buying and selling fractional interest in businesses (not pieces of paper), you will always be AHEAD of the fictional Mr. Market.

Consensus—the Average

Mr. Market is closely related to the Consensus. This is the average of all the ideas, long and short, that "make a market." The price at which you trade, you can consider to be a function of the consensus—at that point. The price is the collective guess about the value of the business at the moment it trades. Your job is simply to determine if that is a GOOD or a BAD price. You don't need to act on it. That's merely what the quoted price is, just like tomatoes or a Big Mac Extra Value Meal. The market, a collective guess consisting of informed and uninformed decisions, makes up the price at the time you trade, between 9:30 and 4pm You'll hear on TV and read on the internet about "consensus forecasts" for earnings. This, too, is the collective guess. The earnings forecast might be very widespread (here are some basic statistics coming into play, and you can imagine the shape of the curve around that point estimate). Are businesses this precise? Not even close, and relying on point estimates OVER simplifies the business an is actually phony precision. You need to think in terms of probability curves, a set of outcomes for earnings—and, more importantly, the "earnings power" of the business. Your mindset should get away from consensus and think more in terms of what the ultimate **earnings power** of a business is. It's actually not complicated to do. We'll discuss this later. And you should burn into your mind when buying ANY business, public or private, that you should have a back-of-the-envelope idea of what the earnings power is. If you can't figure that out, stay away.

Another great quote I'll paraphrase from Ben Graham is that the market is a voting machine in the short run but a weighing machine later. Like many democratic processes, there are votes taking place in the market, with a point estimate of value (the stock price) coming out in much the same way an official becomes an official. Consider close elections between two violently opposing viewpoints. One vote can swing the "price" of one value versus another to a seat in Congress. Serious stuff. But not reflective, necessarily of what happens in the long run, nor even of what a large minority believes. In the long run, the stock market can sort out the value of businesses, often substantially higher or lower than the price at which you entered.

Beware of what is termed the Keynesian beauty contest. The idea, rooted in the old newspaper beauty contests during Keynes's time, is that you are not picking the stock that is the best looking but the one you think others will find best looking. That's a difficult game, though I know some who are good at it.

Handicapping/Probability. This is at its core a probability game.

A great quote from Pierre Simon Laplace,

The most important questions of life are indeed, for the most part, really only problems of probability.

https://www.azquotes.com/author/23554-Pierre_Simon_Laplace

You are handicapping the odds of your company generating the kind of earnings power you have calculated to be likely and then calculating if you're paying an appropriate price for interest in that company, given the valuation you came up with. Sometimes, the ability to sprint is rewarded, when people make temporary mistakes versus what you calculated, you can pounce (like when a company misses the "headline number", gaps down and becomes, temporarily, a great discount.

Does Momentum Work?

We'll discuss "paying up" later. My philosophy is buying good businesses at great prices, and you can think of good business and great price as chart, with one as the X and one as the Y axis. We want to maximize. A great price is a discount on what I calculate the company is worth. Everyone has a different rule of thumb. There's a discipline to "paying up" for a business, and this can go back to something I don't like to do: charting (where you see a stock trading for higher than where it was before and then paying up for it. One mentor of mine called this "follow the follower." You can also call it "greater fool." If you don't have a grounding in what something is worth and you're reliant solely on price movements, you can get in severe trouble. Ask yourself, in this instance, "Is there someone else who will buy it from me, having done the work I SHOULD HAVE DONE (valuing the thing)."

Is the Market Efficient?

Across my career, there's been the argument for and against "market efficiency". In the next chapter, we will talk about notable examples of how the market cannot be totally efficient because they and their track records could not exist. The crux of the efficiency argument is that the stock price represents all things known about the stock at the moment, that that price at that moment is the "right price." I've made mistakes, and I've seen mistakes made—the flash crash back in 2010 had people buying stocks for 0.01 that had traded seconds earlier at 100. That's an extreme case. But the acolytes of Ben Graham and the antecedents of his disciples have proven that the market price isn't necessarily right all the time.

Superinvestors of Graham and Doddsville.

This is a major refutation of the Efficient Market Hypotheses out there. Penned by Buffett himself, it reviews the track records of people who, under the direct or indirect tutelage of Ben Graham, significantly outperformed the market.

Is picking stocks difficult?

Yes, it's difficult. Charlie Munger has said this—if someone tells you it is not difficult, they don't get it. It's, I think, emotionally difficult, because the math is easy, and the terminology is simpler than they make it sound and you do NOT need advanced education, too. I would argue—that it is NOT so difficult that a professional from outside the Wall Street world cannot do it and do it successfully on his or her own if they possess both the contrarian streak and the willingness to do the mental, quantititative and investigative work.

It is complicated, but NOT as complicated as brokerage firms would lead on. Their job is to get you to change your mind, so they invent jargon and concepts that make that happen.

It takes time to learn, but if you are both curious (which you are, you're reading this) and contrarian (ditto), you're equipped.

But it is not impossible, and it is NOT black magic.

And it IS FUN! Stick with me through this book, and you will see why so many of us in the field believe we are hobbyists and not really working, even when at it 80 hours a week.

There are lots of analogies, lots of great war stories, and lots of anecdote, but what's great is you're ultimately buying pieces of fractional businesses. I aim to give you both the toolkit AND the temperament assessment to attempt to do that yourself. OR, at the very least, know how to demystify the business and ask the right questions, much as you'd want to ask your doctor, your attorney or your accountant.

Of course, I am here to help you on the journey as well.

www.convexityhunter.com

CHAPTER 2
WE CAN BE HEROES

At the end of this book, my aim is that you'll be equipped to look at stocks as pieces of business, know the basics of how to value them and know how to keep your framework updated. Luckily, we have a ton of free information out there, including interviews and writings of true deans of the profession.

My Heroes in the business have left behind a reading list for us. Some, like Buffett and Munger and Taleb have videos you can review. You can take the same journey I did and read the books I did.

Borrowing from my civil engineering education and the time I spent around contractors, I will help you understand how to do it yourself. We are NOT building 75-story buildings here, but a basic structure with the help of some heroes of industry.

In this chapter, I'm going to show you the right people to look at: the "professors" I found. The best work to help you understand how to value a business and how to pick a stock comes from observing the greats. If you want to hit home runs, you could hop in a time machine and watch Babe Ruth. We don't need a time machine or even a flux capacitor.

I got interested in the stock market 40 years ago. My uncle traded commodities, so I knew there was something great going on up on Wall Street (a 30-minute ferry ride from my native Staten Island). As a 10-year-old delivering newspapers, for a time, I got the benefit of the Investors Business Daily dropped among the papers I had to deliver. I didn't realize that this error at the newspaper bundling facliity would eventually lead to all of this. But I was fascinated by the numbers and the stories about the different stocks and industries. Owning a slice of a business always appealed to me, and while my parents told me that Wall Street was not suitable for anyone but gamblers, I got the sense that the kind of cars (a 1986 Jaguar) and houses my uncle and his friends had stood in defiance of that, especially given they all seemed relatively level headed and NOT necessarily gambling types. These guys all had quote machines that looked like oversized walkie-talkies. It seemed very cool. Only one of his buddies actually had finished college, but they were ALL doing much better than their parents and my parents and my neighbors.

This was the mid-1980s, and the feeling of the time was that Wall Street was an exciting place. And it was a ferry ride away. This was punctuated for me on Friday nights when an extremely important-looking and sounding guy named Louis Rukeyser hosted other important and serious-sounding people to talk about stocks! Again, being 10,11,12, almost all this Wall Street Week went over my head (though I was lucky enough in 2000 to attend an event honoring Mr. Rukeyser at Carnegie Hall when I DID get exactly what he was doing). Lou was my first hero of investing—because he'd come on Friday evening and host a thinktank of serious portfolio managers and analysts talking about their favorite ideas. They were defending their theses in logical ways. I like it a lot! All this before Crockett and Tubbs came on at 9PM, fighting Vice in Ferraris.

Fast forward to my time in the East Village in engineering school, which I attended merely to impress my future father-in-law (plus, it was free, thanks to the generosity of Peter Cooper, another hero). I'd pick up my then-girlfriend at her campus and hang out in their library, waiting for her. There was the book that cemented it for me: Peter Lynch's ONE UP ON WALL STREET. The bottom line of this book is that you and I can join Mr. Lynch, whose record running Fidelity's Magellan fund was beyond legendary. Pick up a copy of it. I promise, you'll love it. I'm on brian@broadwaycap.com if you want to discuss.

Just around this time, they'd opened the Barnes and Noble with the Starbucks (more on this later) at the Citicorp Tower—a building that actually stands on three columns and has a unique differential equation-driven counterweight up within its roof to counteract potential vibrational damage.

On the 2nd floor of this building, I'd sit and work through my problem sets trying to get through Cooper Union's difficult Civil Engineering degree. To reward myself, I'd read through the 1994 classic "Investment Biker."

Holy Moley!

Jim Rogers, like Peter Lynch, made stock picking—in the case of Mr. Rogers, international stock picking, seem like the most intuitive, most interesting thing in the world. Moreover, in their own ways, they implanted in my brain some great qualitative lessons about digging and going beyond the norm (and beyond our national borders). Read Jim Rogers's books and I bet you'll want to expand your investment horizon internationally, and it is so much easier to do than when he traversed the world on a BMW motorcycle.

As an aside, I spent a year as a 19-year-old trying to get onto Wall Street via the retail stock brokerage route—cold calling 200 phone numbers a day to convince people to take a call with a "senior broker" much the way the film Wall Street depicts it and in the case of one firm I luckily left quickly, the way the film Boiler Room portrayed the industry. Fortunately, for the final 8 months of that year's sojourn, I was hired by one of the oldest firms on the street and would have stayed there but for the acceptance I got at The Cooper Union.

During that brief time, I picked up many great lessons from the senior brokers and analysts (it was, in fact, about 4% of my life up to that point and about a school year), including a crucial one—the CFA Charter offers both a broad and deep view into what professionals should know. While not entirely necessary to achieve success in the industry, the CFA is something about which I am most proud, and its curriculum is worth reviewing even for the novice. What's cool about this is that the CFA Charter was a standard originally encouraged by Ben Graham, who viewed the industry as something that needed professional standards (amen!). Graham was the mentor to many, including (and especially) Warren Buffett.

You are really not an investor until you discover Warren Buffett. I am not only a huge fan but also one who recognizes that there are phases to Buffett's career. He's a teacher and a mentor to so many in our profession, most of us at a distance. Every one of his annual letters can be read at www.berkshirehathaway.com, and thanks to his generosity and that of CNBC, you can watch his annual meeting. By the way, binge watch these with a box of See's Peanut Brittle (https://www.sees.com) and you will come away with a graduate-level understanding of value investing. https://buffett.cnbc.com/annual-meetings/

You can essentially model your career after Buffett, but my warning with him, as with all these heroes, is that you should NOT ape him, and you should understand the evolution of his career as a stock picker, capital allocator and, ultimately, chairman of one of the biggest pools of capital. He is clearly without duplicate, but there are a few facets to the professional Buffett, as I have discovered over the years.

I have a great friend in the industry who often teases me about my affinity toward Buffett, especially since his politics are decidedly different from mine (Buffett is a liberal, supported President Obama and generally approves of government programs I dislike, and I am a staunch libertarian). I remind my buddy that some of the greatest sports heroes are terrible human beings (apologies to my Democrat friends—you are NOT terrible). Emulate these guys ON the field but not necessarily OFF.

A lot of people try to emulate the Buffett of 2023, buying what he's buying NOW, or even the Buffett of 20 to 30 years ago, without recognizing a few major things. 1) he's been dragging around a LOT more capital over these years and—as a result—has far fewer opportunities that would move the needle. They are still there, but some are way to small for Berkshire. He's been telling us this since the 1980s, 2) his cost of capital, given their discipline and size, as well as Berkshire's structure as an insurance company, is typically much lower than the typical investor's—some years it could be considered negative. What appears to be a bargain under that scenario might not be as much of a bargain to an investor with a real cost of capital of say 12-15%, 3) given his size as well as his temperament, he's buying businesses that may ultimately stay in the Berkshire portfolio forever. This isn't necessarily stock picking the way we would want to do it at all times.

Let's look at point 1. Because you and I are smaller than Buffett, we have 100s, if not 1000s, of times the opportunities he has, many of which would meet his 1950s and 1960s Buffett style, and some of which are offshore. This is a major advantage we have. Sure, in the 1950s, Buffett had this kind of opportunity set because he was small; he could walk into the library and read Value Line to pick stocks trading at really low multiples. We have fewer bargains like that, BUT we also have all the financial information at our fingertips. We'll talk about this later under screening.

Once you have gotten to understand how Buffett became Buffett and how he evolved from a seeker of "statistical bargains,."

Where did he get these ideas? Benjamin Graham. The most important book is "The Intelligent Investor". Pause to read that one, and you'll have a lot of timeless tools to do the job of investing. Graham's imprint is thankfully all over our industry because he was the one who did so much to formalize it (and he trained the best of the best)—he was even instrumental in getting the CFA designation started. Had Buffett JUST followed Graham, he would have put together a fantastic record, but likely would NOT be worth over $100 billion. The epiphany that came to Buffett was simply paying up for great businesses at good prices (rather than just buying statistical margins, things that are cheaper than liquidation value). I will point out that depending on the market conditions, you can make money buying statistical bargains (cheap) as well as paying up for great businesses at good prices. These are all qualitative things for now.

Charlie Munger passed away just two weeks before I started working the final draft of this book. An entire set of books could be filled with his wisdom (and one has, Poor Charlie's Almanack, just re-released). If I sat down and wrote about everything I have learned—from afar—listening to Charlie Munger, there could be a whole other book. His sarcasm is unparalleled. His advocation of reading, worldly wisdom, and borrowing from multiple disciplines shapes how people can look at the industry. Oh—and he did NOT go to business school and passed away worth over $2 billion, having been credited (by Buffett himself) with effectively turbocharging Buffett's record. His record, coming into his partnership with Buffett, rivaled that of his future partner but was more concentrated and more volatile (he had the temperament to live with the volatility). His partnership with Buffett is beyond legendary, both within and outside our industry.

A brilliant Harvard-trained lawyer with a 60+ year investment track record managed to conjure phrases like "Mixing raisins with turds" to describe portfolios that consist of large, turdlike problems (you can never dilute the turds with raisins). Two major elements of Munger are relevant to our book. One, he encouraged Buffett—successfully, to consider the intangible elements of valuation (like branding) and to build those into the valuation. Hence, they bought something like See's Candies and later Coca Cola. Second, and I think this is also important, he was known as "The Abominable No Man" by Buffett—an independent sounding board that would NOT kowtow to Buffett (or, seemingly, anyone else) when he knew he was right. In fact, another great Munger expression was, "I'm right, and you're smart, and you'll figure it out."

If you don't have someone like Charlie, I implore you to think what Charlie would say when considering your investment decisions. There is nothing wrong with communicating with the "eminent dead", which is something Munger encouraged, citing his hero Ben Franklin as just one of many in this category.

Having an Abominable No Man for someone as successful as Buffett, in my view, was possibly as important as someone who helped him see the wisdom of moving beyond merely statistical views of value.

Speaking of statistics and—more importantly, probability, I want to mention the master who, for me, ranks among Buffett and Munger for shaping the way I view investing. Nassim N Taleb was the mathematician turned trader turned philosopher, without whose books I would not think about the market the same way. If I could only follow two people in the industry, it would be Munger and Taleb.

I told you I would be giving you homework, but I implore you to read everything he's written. Fooled by Randomness (2001), The Black Swan (2007), Antifragile (2012) and Skin in the Game (2018) are his non-technical books that EVERYONE considering investing in—either the "do it yourself" I'm advocating here or "do it for others" I do professionally.

The first two books will change most people's view of the investment game, removing biases that people have about how probability plays a bigger role in life than people understand (or admit to) and how biases and statistical blindness lead people to view the absence of evidence as evidence of absence.

People tend to build risks into systems without considering that 1) rare events have non-zero probabilities and 2) rare events can potentially have IMPACTS that are non-linear. A lot of this goes back to overconfidence and physics envy that we see in markets. People, because they hadn't seen a black swan, assumed there was none. Until they found one, making all prior models obsolete. Since these two books were written, there's been a cottage industry of calling almost any rare event a "black swan" to justify dumb forecasting.

The major takeaway—you need to build portfolios that can protect against these "fat-tailed" highly destructive things (via insurance—we'll talk about that later), and don't take bets you don't understand. The flip side is that there are rare but highly POSITIVE events that you should be open to—positive convexity. Combining "clipping the tail" with being open to "positive convexity" is a profile around which portfolios and lives should be built.

I implore you to read both of these ASAP.

Then, we move on to Antifragile and Skin in the Game. Antifragile outlines a concept that you should burn into your brain the same way you burned the first two in—you need to build things that ACTUALLY BENEFIT from randomness. View things through the lens of this perspective and look at the world—and your portfolio and investments as fragile, robust or, a third way, antifragile. Skin in the Game teaches us, among many things, to consider actual risk-takers as the true heroes, and those who advise about risk without actually TAKING it are often beneath contempt, since they encourage risk taking but actually don't take risks. This echoes the concept of incentives that Munger often talks about. There are multiple examples in life, and one question

I ask ANY professional is, "What do YOU do for YOUR family?" based on this book. As a civil engineer by training, I love that Taleb and Munger both have cited disincentives historically taken in civil engineering. Look at the company you're buying to see how much management owns, how they are incentivized to generate value for you—and how much skin they have in the game.

Get through the Taleb reading assignment, and it will change your perspective, which is exactly what I want you to do. You'll view risk differently, and you'll think about two of the most important words—Asymmetry and Convexity. You need to think in terms of probabilities and to know that you have to "clip the downside". Think about insurance products you use throughout your life (and at the end of it). You have available to you products in the market such as puts and calls that mimic these products. If you are inclined to be taking a risk you DON'T understand, why take it? To borrow again from Buffett, there are no called strikes, but in investing you can destroy your performance taking one dumb bet (for instance, writing puts to pick up income right before a company files for bankruptcy that you didn't anticipate or writing naked calls on companies taken over).

The question you should have now is, "Once I read these books and watch these videos, which heroes should I follow"? Yes, there is a pantheon of great heroes of investing that I've mentioned, and you'll discover many more. It comes down to your temperament. And here's a trick. Every quarter, the "big guys" file form 13s with the SEC to tell you what they are buying. For me, this is like Christmas four times a year because you can see directly the people you admire buying (and sometimes selling) ideas you like, and you can also mine these for ideas—see more on screening.

Advanced study includes reading the works of Joel Greenblatt and, if you can find them, Seth Klarman. Greenblatt's book "the Little Book that Beats the market" is a classic and gives you a good perspective on how to screen (again, more on screening later). Michael Burry, the short seller and value investor, is worth exploring, as well. Three other great biographies to read would include the autobiography of Leon Cooperman and recent biographies on Jim Simons and Ed Thorp.

STOCK MARKET GENIUS

The Little Book that Beats the Market holds a special place for me because it marries basic tenets of value investing to a quantitative screening process that is appealing. Plus, it's formula is free to use online:

https://www.magicformulainvesting.com.

A word on Activists. In the 1980s, there was a backdrop of "corporate raiders," people who viewed management teams. Names like Carl Icahn and T Boone Pickens (read both of their biographies) came to the fore and taught us about shareholder activism. In our current world, Bill Ackman carried the torch and taught me, through his Wendy's and McDonald's campaigns, a graduate school education on this.

Once you get an eye for what you want to do, you have a trove of investment letters out there that you can read, often for free. Berkshire Hathaway publishes them, as does Munger's Daily Journal, and so did Leucadia National, which operated as a 'mini Berkshire' from 1978 to 2012. (https://www.valuebuddies.com/leucadia.html). Great work from Bill Miller, Howard Marks, and other fund managers is also available.

Later in the book, I'll teach you shortcuts on how to read annual reports, and you'll find management team letters as a Management Team.

I would also encourage you to look at the biographies of Ed Thorp and Jim Simons, both mathematicians like Taleb, who pioneered quantitative methods. Professor Thorp also wrote two great books, one on blackjack and one on the market.

Over time, you'll borrow from each of these greats and many more. I have. In fact, let's talk on brian@broadwaycap.com and compare greats.

Understanding both the statistical and the qualitative is crucial to being a top-it-it-yourself investor as well as a pro. Remember one thing: ALL the investors listed above have a non-1000 batting average. Some have had 50% drawdowns. To a person, they are legends in the field.

This book is about making YOU learn how to become a legend. In Chapter 1, you got the background, and in this Chapter, you got to meet some investment heroes who leave a trail of great ideas to emulate. In the next chapter, you'll be able to identify your own style.

There are SO many great books out there that you can add to your collection.

For a copy of my ever-growing reading list, please reach out. Become a "Book with Legs" like Charlie Munger.

www.convexityhunter.com

CHAPTER 3
QUANTITATIVE / QUALITATIVE STYLE / FUNNEL

To do-figure out your style

At the end of this chapter, you'll be on your way to establishing what kind of investor you are, going beyond the labels: aggressive, conservative, growth, and value. These are labels used by brokerage firms to establish your risk tolerance and your preference for your type of business. I'll take you a few steps deeper because I want you to feel equipped to do some, if not all, of this yourself.

Style

We've already established that you are a contrarian and that you are curious. That was what Chapter 1 was all about. In Chapter 2, I introduced you to a Pantheon of investment legends. The great thing about this business is that no one has a monopoly on great ideas (a term I learned from stockbrokers back in the early 1990s), and no one can really patent their secrets—in fact, all of those investors have published and spoken a LOT what they have done. Collaboration is a fantastic element of this business.

Background

There is indeed a LOT written about the investment business, and this book adds to that. Part of this is because, with very little training, people can pretend to predict the future, however poorly. There are people on television, in newspapers, on the internet, and in newsletters that tell you they can predict the market.

They cannot. In fact, so much ink and so much electronic equivalent of ink is spent trying to predict the future, when time and effort could be spent understanding things probabilistically . So many experts are around, especially as the calendar turns, with their "year-end targets." I get the question all the time, "What will the market do, what will the fed do, what will blah blah do?".

Repeat after me: "I have no (insert expletive if you like) clue."

But Brian, do you have a CFA charter? You have done this for 25 years??? You don't have a prediction?

Nope.

Actually, yup.

The market will be open for 250 or so days. There will be a lot of emotion. People will come in happy, sad, hungover, about to be promoted, about to be fired, elated because of a birth, bummed because of a divorce. They will trade, and they will trade emotionally. People will be angry with a headline and sell an entire position, crushing a stock. People will misread a headline (I've seen this done) and buy the WRONG stock, bidding it up many percentage points before realizing they were wrong.

And the computers—the algorithmic robots that trade—will see this "break out" of a stock and buy more. People might pile on.

I predict that will happen.

Oh, and I predict people will pay too much attention to the Federal Reserve, the War in Ukraine, the Election, etc.

But do I know what the market will do? No. I don't know what I will eat on Saturday for breakfast. Does that bother me? Not at all. Because I know myself. And, I know that legends such as the gentleman in Omaha, his partner who just passed away, and many others don't kid themselves predicting or spend ANY time on it.

Do not hire me if you believe I can predict the market. And, if you're with me and I attempt to, kick me. And avoid people who say they CAN predict the market. (Note, we spend a lot of time trying to avoid things in this book)

Look, if you like predicting things, if you like making a "bet" on what the market would be for next year, make that bet small. It's worse than sports betting. In fact, take the money you would like to bet on what the S&P will do in a year and put that on horses you like. Intellectually, handicapping horses is a lot more like stock investing than people give credit.

Now, isn't buying a stock implicitly making a bet on the future?

AB-SO-LUTE-LY

However, this is educated guessing, not predicting. The more you're educated (not school education but education about the company), the more reasonable the guess. And the more likely you are to build a probability "tree" that considers different possible outcomes and then weights them with some percent "chance".

By owning a stock, you own a piece of the future cash flows of a business. You are assessing whether or not that company will generate profits sufficient to justify the price you paid, and using a "hurdle rate" to discount those future predicted flows for uncertainty. Effectively, you're inverting. The price is Y, and the cash flows from now until the end of time are X. Y is a function of X. The more you understand the business, the more you can understand the earnings power of the business, the X, so you feel comfortable paying Y or less. You are not betting on what the central bank will do or what the retail sales number for October will do (although don't entirely dismiss relevant factors in macroeconomics or geopolitics; they figure into the setting). You're making a bet on two things - 1) the company's ability to deliver earnings power commensurate with the price you paid for it, and 2) your analysis of the price you paid for it.

Do you have the temperament to know if you're getting a bargain when you go into a store? You have knowledge of what a wool suit or a six-pack of Sam Adams should sell for. Stocks are somewhat the same thing, but underlying the stock is a set of future cash flows.

You need to have the guts to go into the stock market some days and DO NOTHING, just browse. None of the prices line up with what you want to pay? Wait until they do. As Buffett says, "There are no called strikes". You need to go in some days when the "market is down x100 points" and buy. You need to have the style to buy when they're down and add when they are down more. To do this, you can't worry too much about market predictions because you DO NOT KNOW THE FUTURE. What you need to do is define your style and establish your

Style is tied to your temperament (you're a contrarian; you've read me for this many pages! You're curious; ditto!) and is a function of your risk tolerance.

A GUARANTEE!

I cannot make guarantees about the future other than that from time to time, you will lose money in a position. There are the unrecognized losses (stock goes down, but you don't sell, and then it recovers) and the recognized ones (you sold—at a loss). You will have both. 100% of the time, you'll enter a stock at a slight loss, because of commissions and/or spread. If you cannot handle that basic assertion that you will lose on a large percentage of your trades (30-40%), you should not do this yourself.

So here you go: are you conservative or aggressive in your approach to risk? That depends. What is your "uncle point," as Taleb defines it—the point at which you can't take any more (think about the bully in Christmas Story twisting Ralphie's buddy's arm).

And do you define yourself as a growth investor or a value investor?

Can you deal with fear? Can you buy something when the market consensus is against you? Can you buy against a trend? Can you buy index puts?

Let's keep going.

Growth/Value

This kind of dichotomy is one we should dispense with right away. At what point is a growth stock a value stock? Is there a spectrum like ROY-G-BIV? Is there a bright line at which you instantly stop emulating Charlie Munger and start emulating Cathie Wood?

Value vs growth is not helpful in the context of defining a style. Yes, some companies grow faster than others on both the top (sales/revenue) and bottom (earnings, cash flow) basis. But sometimes, these companies are "cheap"—we'll come up with a framework for figuring that out later. So, you're buying a software company that has had and looks to have compounding earnings power, but you're buying it at a PE multiple lower than that of a tired, old, low-growth auto manufacturer. Are you a value investor? Are you a growth investor? Is this DUMB? Labels can be dumb.

Buffett has said so well, "Value and growth is joined at the hip." And Munger has talked about all investing being value investing—paying for something less than it's worth. Graham has gone so far as to say that anything that isn't buying stuff at a discount, with a MARGIN OF SAFETY, speculation, not investing. There is a LOT of speculation out there. And, to your advantage, there are STILL, a full 90 YEARS after the publication of Security Analysis, people who don't care what a stock is "worth"; they just buy.

Are you a long-term investor?

Here's an interesting question. When you are buying a stock, you're necessarily and contractually entitled to be participating in the future of the business. Given the market for many companies is liquid, especially for smaller investors, and transaction costs are very low to nil, even for the smallest, there is the ability to trade in and out of the ownership position, capturing small gains as the market fluctuates. As I noted at the beginning of this book, I am not a lot of things (including your accountant), but what I can say is that while trading like this can be fun, and if you're good at it, profitable on a gross basis, the transaction cost that you likely cannot avoid is the short term treatment of capital gains. The government actually dissuades you from short-term trading—or, put another way, becomes a BIGGER partner in your gains (they don't even thank you, and can't even plug potholes). So take that into consideration.

At the heart of what I do is thinking about the following, a question my mentor Rick put into my head—"does the value of the business you're considering really change by 3-4-5% in a day?" The price does and can. And sure, there is often some news that can destroy a business in a day (or double its value, like discovering oil or getting FDA approval for a drug). But, generally, a 2-3% move in the market price of something is less related to the value of that thing and more related to the often-frenetic nature of the market.

What about trading?

We'll learn more about this later, but the market can give you tremendous opportunities, short-term, to own great businesses at sometimes temporarily stupid prices. When we talk about portfolio management and investment sizing rules of thumb, I'll share some of my ideas.

Trading takes a special kind of temperament. Are you a trader?

At this point, you've discovered your interests, dispelled the concept of growth versus value, and developed a different framework for considering aggressive versus conservative approaches. You can go into the stock selection process with somewhat of a "clean slate," knowing that you can do it, that many have done it different ways (and succeeded), and that you have a sense of the toolkit you'll need. In the next section, we're going to look at how to narrow down the field and how to ask the crucial questions not just of yourself, should you choose to do it yourself, but also of your advisor.

And if you want a gut check, I'm around at brian@broadwaycap.com.

CHAPTER 4
GO WITH WHAT YOU KNOW / INDUSTRY SELECTION

So far, we've established that you're both contrarian and curious enough to embark on a do-it-yourself journey. We had an overview of the greats of investing. In the last chapter, we gave you an overview of how to consider investing styles. Now, we are getting into the actual fun piece: stock picking.

Company types

This is where the fun begins. A shortcut to figuring out what to buy is extremely useful, given there are over 6000 publicly traded companies in the US and Canada with market capitalizations over $25 million. And that doesn't include the thousands more that we can look for abroad (remember Jim Rogers, the Investment Biker).

What kind of companies do you want to work with and analyze? Buy what you know is a good piece of advice borrowed from Peter Lynch. You are a consumer; you may be an employee or entrepreneur (or both). You don't even need to leave your home to determine a bunch of businesses with which you are familiar. I'm typing this on an Apple MacBook (AAPL) using Microsoft Word (MSFT) and Adobe Acrobat (ADBE). I'm looking at one of my four trading laptops, all powered by NVIDIA (NVDA) and AMD chips. You may be reading this book on Amazon's (AMZN) Kindle. Have a cup of Starbucks

(SBUX) coffee, and we'll start the road to picking stocks. All of these are great companies. They may NOT be great stocks. We'll cover that distinction later.

If you're a physician, you have domain knowledge about medicine, medical equipment, and insurance that sets you apart from others. If you're an engineer, you have similar domain knowledge in multiple fields, like construction, maybe metals and mining. You can use these to your advantage.

I like to start with where I am ignorant (we all are, and if you think you're not, go back to the temperament chapter). I turn 50 this year. I know what I don't know. I also know where I can get killed. I tend to look at the industry groups and start from there, crossing out groups where I don't think I have an edge. Some industries I cross out are actually REALLY interesting, like biotech, but I'm not sure I'd ever get a good edge there.

The S&P500 has 11 industry groups: Communications Services, Consumer Discretionary, Consumer Staples, Energy, Financials, Health Care, Industrials, Information Technology, Materials, Real Estate, and Utilities.

You don't have to be an expert on all of them, or even half of them, to have a more than satisfactory return. In fact, all you had to do the month I was born was to put $10,000 with an obscure company in Omaha, and you'd be fine. Or, 20 years ago, $10,000 in a bookseller run by Jeff Bezos. Note how Forrest Gump did fine with shares of a fruit company (for those who don't get the reference, his friend Lieutenant Dan bought the Apple IPO for them).

For instance, if I were starting from the top of a funnel, I'd rule out Financials, Health Care, Real Estate and Utilities. Have I made money in each of these sectors? Absolutely. Do I possess some edge in some of them? I think so. But there are nuances to each of these industries where I feel like my time is better spent and my work better rewarded in other industries. For instance, I spent a lot of time professionally studying energy IT and consumer staples. You may be a physician or a nurse. Don't rule out Health Care. A buddy of mine had a part time oncology nurse for a mom; on a modest middle class salary she was a multi-millionaire picking biotech stocks with ZERO insider information! You might be a whiz at understanding bank balance sheets and net interest margins—keep financials in there. Reduction is getting rid of industries and companies where you don't think you can develop an edge (we'll talk more about what that is throughout the book, but suffice it to say that it involves the ability AND desire to get differential information and insight). Buffett has said you ought to think you have just "20 punches", 20 big ideas across your life to make a huge difference; there are 300x that across just the US and Canada!

Funnels

In case you haven't noticed, I like speaking in analogies. When I was in engineering school, in the Soil Mechanics lab, we had sieves to sort soil sizes—think of the guys panning for gold in the movies for the final step. Here, we're sorting by industry group.

Those are the "big rocks". Munger and Buffett discuss the "too hard pile." I want you to think of "too hard pile" as a reject filter. The electrical engineers would talk about "filters," whereby noise would be filtered out of an electrical signal. You want to filter noise as well.

In this funnel, the top of which looks like "all publicly traded companies in the US and Canada over $25 million market cap", as we established, we had over 6000, actually 6300 names.

The way we narrow down your stock selection to a bite-sized group. Time to build the funnel.

When I started doing this myself in engineering school, Yahoo Finance was in its infancy, but it was a good enough screener. You don't need a Bloomberg terminal (though I love those) or even an online screening subscription (I'll list my favorite later) to build your universe and get some basic ideas of where these companies trade valuation-wise.

Here we are 25 years later, and we can do the same thing with Yahoo Finance that I discussed earlier.

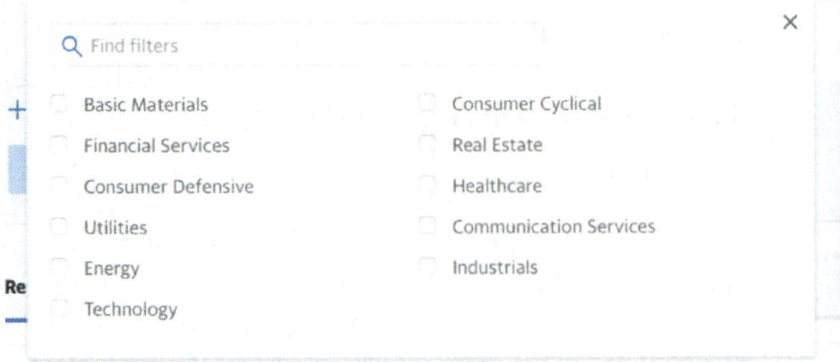

Source: www.yahoo.com

For the sake of this discussion, let's see what universe we would get if we just looked at US Consumer Defensive stocks. There are 682 of these per Yahoo.

These stocks range from Walmart (WMT), with a $415 billion market capitalization, to penny stocks like Purple Beverage Company (PPBV), with a market cap as low as $2400.

Remember, we've sorted for Location (United States) and Sector (Consumer Defensive), but didn't put a lower bound on market capitalization. Let's arbitrarily put $10 million just to see how much the universe narrows. As of December 2023, there are 473 of these (including some duplicates for companies like Nestle that have multiple classes of shares).

Note the top 10 of these are truly household names, where everyone has an opinion because everyone knows the company's products. Walmart, Procter and Gamble, Nestle, Costco, L'Oreal, Coca-Cola, FEMSA (a household name in Latin America because it controls a Coca-Cola Bottler, shares of Heineken Breweries, and a chain of convenience stores), Pepsi, Philip Morris International (tobacco), and Anheuser Busch InBev.

A couple of observations here. These are all companies that one could consider "great." They dominate their categories, are absolutely necessary to their customers (sadly, including tobacco, which took my Dad too early) and have economies of scale that can certainly deter competition. Financially, most of them support dividends and, because of their cash flows, balance sheets and income strength, attract credit ratings that enable them to raise lower-cost debt (for the most part). For the non-enterprising investor, a portfolio of these 10 companies would be easy to analyze, easy to understand and probably conservative to own from a definitional standpoint. We will get into all these attributes later and how to assess them. Their sheer size, however, makes the opportunity for "multi-bagger" opportunities (in which the stocks can increase 10,100x) nearing impossible. Think this way: Walmart has a market capitalization (market cap) of $414 billion. To get a 10-bagger out of that, you need two things to happen - 1) you need to buy a DeLorean, find plutonium and a Doc named Brown, and head back to Arkansas, or 2) you need to see Walmart's market cap rise to $4.14 Trillion, which would represent a market cap equal to about 15% of the entire US economy. Intuitively, you find that somewhat absurd. Later, we'll talk about valuation, and you'll understand WHY this is absurd (and it's a great way to think about valuation—market cap/GDP). Suffice it to say that in consumer staples, these top 10 are in the top 10 because they actually provide top 10 dominance in some way in their categories.

A few more questions will come to mind here, and it's more pronounced in other sectors than in more mundane "defensive stocks." Why do some companies have trillion-dollar valuations when they produce less revenue or earnings than Walmart? Why are some companies in the staples category trading at lower or higher multiples than Walmart? Is Sam Adams possibly worth more than Anheuser? What about Amazon as a "killer" of Walmart or even Target? All of these questions, and more, dear reader, will be addressed later. And it speaks to the fact that "great stock" may not equal "great business," and another concept we'll discuss is called "priced to perfection." Later, we can go through different valuation methods, both popular and more esoteric (but more useful), that you can use to "triangulate" the value.

Now that we know how to narrow down into sector and industry, and we know we can do it for free, the next steps will be to figure out if they are worth buying. You're going to know what questions to ask if someone pitches you a stock tip, what to ask your advisor when you see things in your portfolio, and even have the toolkit to figure it out.

CHAPTER 5
COMPANY SELECTION

The funnel is not the only way to find stocks, but I promise you if you get into the discipline of ruling out sectors and industries where you aren't fully comfortable, I promise, the job will be easier.

That's really what this is about—sifting out areas where you aren't comfortable. You can actually make a fortune investing if you stick with what you know rather than try to be a generalist and over-diversifying. Certainly, think about the richest families you know personally. Many of them became rich from one specific industry, one specific PRIVATE business. Consider some of the great billionaires in the public markets like Bezos, Gates, Buffett (ok, he got rich running money), Munger, etc from one public company. One of my favorite local companies, Hess, made billionaires out of its founding family.

Aside from people I personally know in the finance industry, I have met people worth 8 figures (over $10 million) from real estate (tons of them), education (multiple), convenience stores, and transportation (multiple). The expression, put all your eggs in one basket and WATCH THAT BASKET was not lost on these people. Many of these friends would hit me if I told them to "diversify away from that business." I've had clients worth $ 50 million plus put some "play money" in the stock market but still have 98% of their net worth stay in the core business. If it's good enough for them, it's good enough for you.

But wait, you say (correctly)—in those situations, the private businesses especially, those people have a large degree of control over the business. In the stock market you do NOT. One notable example of a founder getting fired at a public company was, of course, Steve Jobs, and I've seen that happen in private businesses for regulatory reasons, but you're right. You should have more than just one stock in the portfolio because you don't have control; you're a minority shareholder, and even if you've found the "next Apple," you need to have a few businesses in the portfolio because you will be wrong.

I met a guy who was smart enough to buy Apple back in 2000—enough that it made a difference (you'll find that many people make this claim, but he was telling the truth). The difference between a braggart and this gentleman is the $4.5 million New York City townhouse he was able to buy about 15 years ago with the proceeds on an upper-middle-class salary. His portfolio in 2000 was not ALL apple, and, had it been, he may have been able to buy 10 townhouses with the loot. But he diversified by a factor of 10---he had 10 good ideas in that portfolio, and in the year 2000, it was HIGHLY speculative, albeit correct, to bet on Steve Jobs's return to Apple as the catalyst that would drive the returns he later enjoyed.

For perspective, he bought the house around 2018. He bought the Apple shares in his mid-30s in 2000, about $100k worth, in a portfolio he figured had about $1mm at that point—"Apple plus some blue chips from my IRA and money my grandma left me." 18 years later, Apple had run from the equivalent of $0.80 to over 40—a 50-bagger. That house is probably worth 3x of what he paid for it back in 2018. The Apple kept pace and actually beat that return.

I digress. Remember, there are 9 other names in his portfolio he didn't mention that did "okay". And—again—Apple was by no means, even with Steve Jobs, a statistical bargain. In fact, this was before the iPhone, the iPad, the iPod and even the credibility that comes from the dominance of these kinds of markets. Dell was actually the top brand, and no serious business person used Macs at that point. I recall being in a brokerage office listening to a high-performing yet wrong institutional salesman yelling at the TV because a black-turtleneck-clad Steve Jobs was talking about the latest Macs. "That guy is selling colorful computers to artists. This is BS." Again—I love many institutional brokers and consider some to be brothers and sisters. But, 26-year-old me should have ignored that broker. Bet against these types.

The flip side is it's not as easy as looking at your CNBC and saying, "I like the cut of that guy's gib/turtleneck," and plunking down 100k. The ability to pick 50 baggers and even 10 baggers is beyond mere "buying cheap," though that is part of it. The market may not be totally efficient, but it will take more than just paying 8x trailing earnings to get a 50 baggger. What my friend stumbled upon was something Munger showed Buffett—there are intangible factors worth paying up for. And there are Steve Jobs circa 1976 types RIGHT NOW building another Apple with 1976 Steve Wozniak and 2000-vintage Steve Jobs coming back to create things that run from 78c to 180, picking up Buffett and Munger along the way (they were, incidentally, buying around the time my pal was selling to buy the townhouse!)

I digress again. I want to get you back to finding your sweet spot through the funnel. Lurking in the funnel is the next Walmart of 1974 (the year I was born and the best-performing stock since then, over 570k%). Imagine—all my grandfather had to do the year I was born was buy some of Sam Walton's (whom he admired from afar—we didn't have one in Staten Island) shops. Incidentally, my buddy should have bought Monster Beverage alongside Apple in 2000 (it compounded over 101k% as of the beginning of this year).

Screening, the way I'm showing you, enables you to narrow down a field of stocks you can work with for your own portfolio. As we go through the discipline of narrowing down these kinds of ideas, you'll also be able to go "the other way," from specific to broad, when someone gives you an idea. For instance, you may hear a pitch at a cocktail party, or barbecue, or from your advisor. Having gone through the discipline of screening through sectors, industries, subindustries and stocks, you'll know what questions to ask and what key performance indicators you can think about when formulating a buy or sell thesis. You can dazzle them with your investigative abilities.

As I write this, Barrons (worth the subscription for the ideas you'll get every Saturday) has released its 10 top ideas for the year.

Let's revisit the S&P500 industry groups we discussed earlier.

I like to visit bargain shops. Not necessarily Dollar General but places like Maine's famous Marden's, a passion I share with my mother-in-law. This place offers fishing equipment, books, and clothes—all items from stores that didn't succeed or that couldn't move the merchandise, available at incredibly discounted prices, often just a fraction of their original cost. I like to look through the 52-week low list (more on THIS later, too) for these sorts of things and at the worst performing ideas.

Thanks to my amazing father-in-law's foresight, we can visit his house in Maine for annual trout and bass fishing. In his final interview, Charlie Munger compared this business to trout fishing. It's enjoyable. You will never master it, but you will get better and better each time. You can do it with the simplest of tools, but the tools you can employ (spinner versus fly rod, flies vs. nightcrawlers, different lures of different types) are nearly infinite, and NONE is guaranteed to work every time.

Our job is about going to the right body of water, the right trout stream, under the right conditions. To follow the analogy, we should consider we want to "catch a limit" of brook trout. Brook trout are my code word for great stocks for the portfolio. By narrowing down the sectors and industry groups, we're picking the places where we are most likely to be successful.

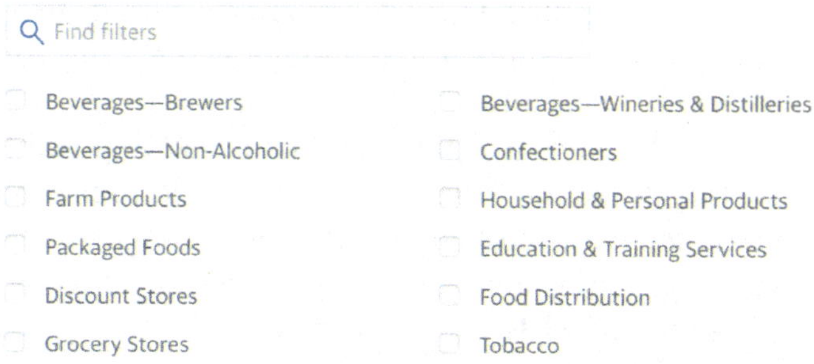

Back to Yahoo's free stock screener. The place where I began. (Again, I'll show you the advanced tools later—I promise—but this one is good enough.) You don't need a $1200 fly reel with a $1000 rod to catch great fish, and you can use this to narrow down the pool of great candidates.

Defensives include the following industries:

We're trying to narrow down areas where we believe we can have an edge and make money.

For fun, let's look at areas where I've enjoyed studying and where I have made money. Beverages and Packaged Foods. What does the Beverage universe look like? There are 93 companies there with a market cap of >$10 million, ranging from Coca-Cola (KO) at the high end to Big Rock Brewery Inc. (BRBMF) at the low. One thing is immediately evident to me—some of these companies trade very little volume per day. If you're trying to build a reasonably-sized investment in a company, 200 shares a day of a $1.00 stock might not cut it, no matter how great the company is. Let's come up with a heuristic. 10,000 shares a day. That narrows the field to 48 companies.

Those are just US-listed companies and JUST beverages. It's quite a playground to find "the next Monster." Consider that everyone needs to stay hydrated and that right now, someone is possibly making something that will emulate Monster (note there are two Formula 1 teams, including a multi-year championship one sponsored by Monster competitor Red Bull, so there is possibly room for more energy drinks.)

Packaged Foods with market caps over $10 million and trading volume over 10k adds another 75 companies to the expanding universe of US stocks we can work through.

That list is topped by Nestle's ADR (American Depository Receipt, meaning you can buy Swiss stock in the US) and Kraft Heinz (KHC). These brands are ubiquitous. You cannot avoid Nestle's or Kraft Heinz. My university-aged son once (at age 5) made his great uncle, the older brother of his grandpa, return to the grocery store specifically for Heinz Ketchup. I have a photo of the young man at Berkshire's annual here:

Note the two fellas in the "Wiener Mobile" and my son.

The smallest trading under the symbol PETZ is TDH Holdings. Until this writing, I didn't know what PETZ does.

TDH Hldgs

Company

TDH Holdings, Inc. **engages in the development, manufacture, and distribution of pet food products**. Its product categories include pet chews, dried pet snacks, wet canned pet food, dental health snacks, and baked pet biscuits. It operates through the Petfood Sales and Restaurant Business segments.

Again, by law—one of the BEST laws the US produced, these companies have to put out annual reports.

You now have 48+75—123 annual reports we can look at. What I would do next is rank them in some kind of order in terms of a few metrics I'll tell you about later; one guide you can think about comes from the Magic Formula book, in which return on capital and enterprise value/EBIT are the measures considered. Let's not skip ahead too much YET. I promise we'll discuss these later.

Here's the point--

This part is easy and fun.

You can replicate what we've done in this chapter, FOR FREE, step by step, for industries in which you have an edge and/or an interest. Here's my thought on edge. It starts with interest. If you're interested in something about a company and its industry, you'll develop a framework for analyzing its nuances. For instance, if you love restaurants (which I do) and specifically things like Starbucks (I do), you can get into that industry analysis pretty quickly and understand the key metrics/performance indicators important to the management and shareholders by reading the annual reports critically.

STARBUCKS.

I love coffee. I even live part-time in one of the great coffee regions of the world, Panama, and have been lucky enough to visit coffee houses in Costa Rica and Colombia.

My father-in-law's firm was involved in the construction of the Barnes and Noble (86th and Broadway) that brought the first Starbucks to New York. I spent the back half of engineering school and most of my CFA charter studying in a Starbucks in Manhattan. To say that my blood is not red but a dark roast may not be an exaggeration.

Starbucks lives within the Consumer Cyclical sector, specifically in the industry group "Restaurants."

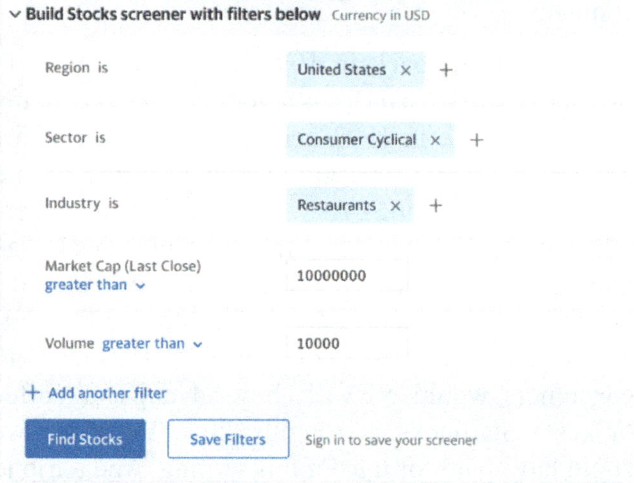

What else is there?

The top one, the market cap, is McDonald's. Right after Starbucks, which is number 2, is Chipotle. I still have the very cool Chipotle IPO t-shirt (ChIPOtle—get it) I received when McDonald's spun it out. By the way, spin-outs are often an incredible way to make money. Note that McDonald "incubated" Chipotle, and that company is now a $62 billion market cap thing in its own right! Pay special attention to spun out businesses, because they often represent a great opportunity to make money.

Anyway, note that Starbucks (SBUX) has a $109 billion market capitalization and trades 7.5 million shares daily. At $96.75, the stock has traded between $89 and $115 over the past 52 weeks (as of this writing, December 2023). These are the stats available to us now. Nothing tells us if it's a buy, sell or hold. And, yes, I reiterate that I LOVE the company.

As an aside, back in 1994, I was introduced to Starbucks stock (SBUX) as a young broker (I got my "Series 7" back in 1993 because, with $500 of my girlfriend's money and that license, I figured I could get into stock picking). As with Apple in 2000, where a know-it-all broker denounced the turtleneck-clad Steve Jobs, this time, a 70+-year-old salesman told a younger broker that her Starbucks stock pick AND her choice in coffee were flawed, that New York consumers would NEVER buy $4 cups of coffee (Yikes!) Starbucks is roughly 200x the price we could have paid for it as of this writing. And a trip to Starbucks in 1994 in New York City

With restaurants, as with beverages, you see familiar companies and brands among the top market cap names and even toward the lower end.

Why do I recommend looking both at beverages and restaurants to start? 1) everyone knows these industries, 2) their products are easy to track, 3) you can "channel check" them easily by visiting them (try this at a nuclear utility or at a bitoin "mine"!), 4) there are brands that are within the 48 restaurants or the 123 or so beverage companies that could be "the next" Coke or Monster or Starbucks. Right now, a new Chipotle is being hatched within a McDonald's or via private equity. I can remember the thrill of getting my first taste of Seattle coffee when they opened across from the Cooper Union on Astor

Place—and my pal and I were admonished for saying "large" instead of "grand-ay." Think about your first experience with the brand.

Here's Starbucks's IPO internal announcement (which corresponds roughly to the month I graduated high school). Had someone bought $1000 worth of Starbucks stock for my graduation present—or if I'd been smart enough to take my graduation checks and buy, I'd have roughly $361,000. I used that money, about 8 months later, to start dating my current wife. She's about the only thing better than a 361 bagger. Also, I'd own just over 3760 shares, so I'd be receiving about $8000 a year in dividends.

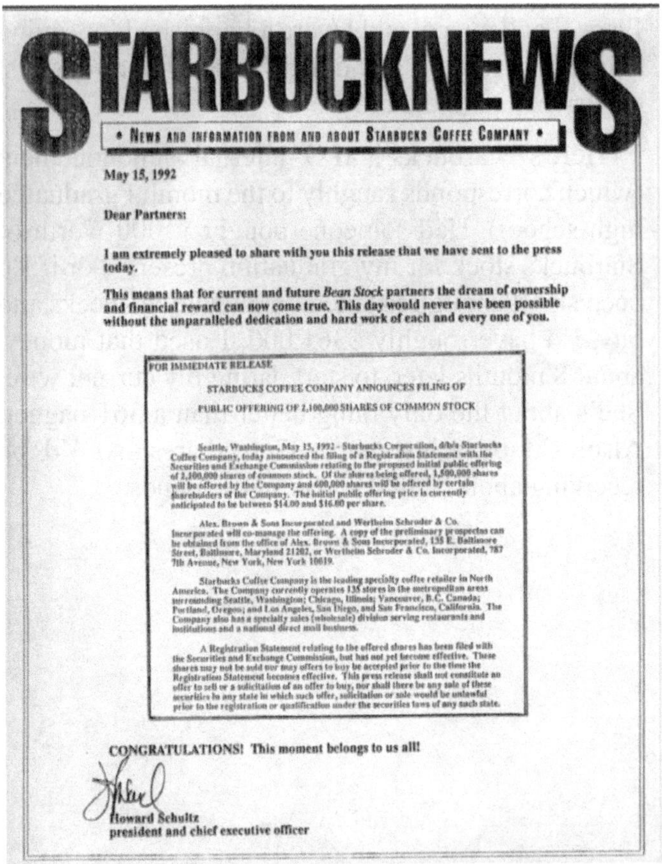

STARBUCKNEWS

• NEWS AND INFORMATION FROM AND ABOUT STARBUCKS COFFEE COMPANY •

May 15, 1992

Dear Partners:

I am extremely pleased to share with you this release that we have sent to the press today.

This means that for current and future *Bean Stock* partners the dream of ownership and financial reward can now come true. This day would never have been possible without the unparalleled dedication and hard work of each and every one of you.

FOR IMMEDIATE RELEASE

STARBUCKS COFFEE COMPANY ANNOUNCES FILING OF

PUBLIC OFFERING OF 2,100,000 SHARES OF COMMON STOCK

Seattle, Washington, May 15, 1992 - Starbucks Corporation, d/b/a Starbucks Coffee Company, today announced the filing of a Registration Statement with the Securities and Exchange Commission relating to the proposed initial public offering of 2,100,000 shares of common stock. Of the shares being offered, 1,500,000 shares will be offered by the Company and 600,000 shares will be offered by certain shareholders of the Company. The initial public offering price is currently anticipated to be between $14.00 and $16.00 per share.

Alex. Brown & Sons Incorporated and Wertheim Schroder & Co. Incorporated will co-manage the offering. A copy of the preliminary prospectus can be obtained from the office of Alex. Brown & Sons Incorporated, 135 E. Baltimore Street, Baltimore, Maryland 21202, or Wertheim Schroder & Co. Incorporated, 787 7th Avenue, New York, New York 10019.

Starbucks Coffee Company is the leading specialty coffee retailer in North America. The Company currently operates 135 stores in the metropolitan areas surrounding Seattle, Washington; Chicago, Illinois; Vancouver, B.C. Canada; Portland, Oregon; and Los Angeles, San Diego, and San Francisco, California. The Company also has a specialty sales (wholesale) division serving restaurants and institutions and a national direct mail business.

A Registration Statement relating to the offered shares has been filed with the Securities and Exchange Commission, but has not yet become effective. These shares may not be sold nor may offers to buy be accepted prior to the time the Registration Statement becomes effective. This press release shall not constitute an offer to sell or a solicitation of an offer to buy, nor shall there be any sale of these securities in any state in which such offer, solicitation or sale would be unlawful prior to the registration or qualification under the securities laws of any such state.

CONGRATULATIONS! This moment belongs to us all!

Howard Schultz
president and chief executive officer

My mission is to find the next one like this—and it can be your mission, too.

So far, we've looked at two industry groups that are simple and easy to understand. When we get to the chapter on analyzing annual reports, you'll see familiar things—pictures of beer bottles, coffee mugs, burgers. Starbucks even has a cool photo of a tractor pulling a trailer full of delicious coffee beans in an idyllic coffee finca setting.

I'm going to stay in restaurants for a bit more—why not?

Chain restaurants, I have found, are a fantastic place to make money and KNOW why you made money because they are simple businesses. They can also get in tremendous trouble due to over-expansion. Krispy Kreme, known for amazing donuts, suffered from overexpansion and oversaturation during the earlier part of my career. In my early lifetime, I had two absolute favorite spots, Howard Johnson and Roy Rogers. In the 1980s, they were ubiquitous because they were EXCELLENT. The last HoJo's disappeared about 5 years ago. Roy Rogers, once one of the top chains in the nation, was—last I checked—trying to resurrect.

How businesses fail is an absolutely fascinating thing for me, and understanding how a business can be destroyed by bad management, mismanagement, competition and a variety of other factors both within and outside management control are—in my view—even MORE important than understanding the ingredients for success. Destroy a business in your mind. Come up with as many likely scenarios for this, and then come up with a few more. For instance, with fast food, assume they'll over-expand, that management will have tired menus, and that competition will rise.

FAST FOOD

Fast food restaurants have attracted activism over the years, and both Wendy's and McDonald's attracted letters from Bill Ackman, the famous activist and value investor who runs Pershing

Square. At roughly the same time I moved from the sell side (brokerage) to the buy side (investment management), Ackman launched campaigns against both companies. We'll cover both campaigns later, but Ackman's presentations (I was lucky enough to go to the McDonald's one live and to the Wendy's HQ right after he launched) strike at the heart of what can be analyzed at restaurants and what can possibly go wrong.

Through my analysis of fast food and beverages, I improved my capability for cross-sectional industry analysis. Wendy's and McDonald's do not operate in isolation; they face both emerging and declining competition.

They also had supply chains to consider. You cannot make a burger meal without multiple inputs, including wheat, potatoes, beef, milk (for cheese), tomatoes, lettuce, high fructose corn syrup, and potatoes. Energy is a consideration to transport the stuff (and make it), as are the fertilizers required to grow cattle into beef or milk cows for the cheese. Before –or as--you start to think about Burger King taking share from McDonalds, you are wise to think about the entire chain that creates the product. Luckily, a lot of the raw materials are either made by publicly traded suppliers (that must talk publicly) and/or are traded commodities, such as wheat, beef, oil, gas, etc.

Competition is extremely important to analyze. In fact, I will spend the entirety of the next chapter on it.

A lot of things in investing can go wrong, not just competition. Commodity businesses, such as energy, mining, fertilizers, and transportation, can endure pronounced cycles, and the stocks can trade with even more hyperactivity.

I'm going to look at two hypercyclical and often interrelated things: transportation and energy.

Transportation—things that move.

PLANES, trains, automobiles was another fantastic holiday film. Each of these is a high-profile industry about which everyone has an opinion. They can be extremely tricky industries in which to invest. I had spent a lot of time in both aviation and automobiles (technically, these are part of the consumer cyclical industry, and not part of industrials) and less time in trains because in a frequent bout of "working on" a series of stocks but not yet coming to a conclusion—some call this "analysis paralysis," I didn't finish my work on the rails right before Berkshire bought the BNSF. However, I have also dedicated considerable time to studying maritime industries and ships and acquiring insights on how to navigate within that realm.

Airlines-bankruptcies, 2020

Airlines are a terrible business, selling a commodity—a seat—that goes bad the moment it takes off empty. An entire generation of Buffett followers eschewed buying airline stocks because of his difficult time making a position in USAir work many years ago and his assessment that the industry was basically in the "too hard" pile. It can be, and as with many industries, it has nuances that can make it way too difficult to be worth the time (autos have this flavor, as do many commodity companies). I and my clients have made money multiple times in this industry and have been studying it closely since 2005. Then, as a new analyst, I was sent to see JetBlue unveil its second "fleet type," the Embraer. It has been very difficult, and you're often forced to buy when others are selling heavily. We'll spend more on this later. Suffice it to say that the industry in the US consolidated significantly coming into and after the global financial crisis of 2008, effectively reducing the number of "network carriers" from 6 to 3—Delta, United and American remained while Northwest, Continental and USAir were merged, with the deals announced in 2008, 2010 and 2015. I tracked these mergers closely. Buffett ended up with positions in 4 carriers but sold—smartly in 2020. However, this was a buying opportunity for the small fund that I started in early 2000. I promise to share these stories later.

I would suggest reading about three people in the industry who can give you a deep understanding of how to make money in it. The first is Herb Kelleher, founder of Southwest. The second is Michael O'Leary, the man who built Ryanair, named for Tony Ryan, its founder, about whom you should also read (there is a great biography of him as well). The bottom line is cost and reliability. I think that consolidation has helped the investment case for the industry, CARS.

I love cars and come from a family that loves cars. I've owned vintage British cars (and have the scars and bills and Saturdays spent looking for parts to prove that) and have had 7 BMWs in a row. I go to Formula 1 races with my son, and we watch them together across the ocean thanks to our F1 subscriptions. As someone who grew up around cars, I naturally gravitated toward the industry and its supply chain.

Ships offer a tangible asset, massive demand, a tie into global trade, massive cyclicality and hyperactive stock trading. Clean and dirty tankers for transporting oil products—refined and crude oil to refineries are joined by LNG tankers and LPG tankers. Bulk carriers carry commodities ranging from coal and iron ore for steelmaking to grains. Container ships, which revolutionized the transportation of products to market, provide intermodality—an innovation that, in itself, transformed the flow of goods. This is an amazingly fascinating business to cover and must be observed from the perspective not only of the product supply/demand characteristics but also from the new building and from the credit cycle. These businesses can take off as proxies for the underlying commodity tightness, as we saw in 2006-2008, and it ended badly.

What unites all of these is the cyclicality of both the companies and the stocks.

Energy

I have had multiple adventures in energy, specifically hydrocarbons, which has the three subcategories of oil, gas and coal. Naturally, one would think that these inputs to transportation (the largest input into commercial aviation, for instance) are worth exploring deeply (ha), and the complexity of oil, gas and coal is amazingly high, from understanding exploration to extraction to refining and considering all the geopolitical elements attached.

Energy is massively controversial, and everyone has an opinion about the "price of gas," the "Middle East," the environment, electric vehicles and—no matter how under or misinformed, there is NEVER a lack of people willing to share those opinions.

Me, I've studied the industry closely since the late 1990s and have been on "both sides," long and short, from the largest integrateds (such as Exxon and Chevron) to the smallest explorers and service companies. Do not let the fact that there are really two commodities keep you from understanding that this is an incredibly complicated industry—crude oil and natural gas (coal is a separate animal, and I've spent less time on it).

Ultimately, these are commodity businesses. Branded gasoline and even branded airlines are in a fight to the end with a product where differentiation isn't really.

Figuring out moats is the most important element to understanding how your business can ultimately be a good stock. Brand businesses, like Starbucks and McDonald's, sell commodity products (coffee and burgers) but elevate this to an experience and domination that are difficult---but not impossible—to assail. Information technology, with patents and trade secrets galore (and billions of R&D spending), has many stories of dominance being unseated—note

Apple versus all the incumbents in 2000 or Apple versus Nokia.

In the next chapter, we'll talk much more in-depth about assessing competitive advantage.

CHAPTER 6
COMPETITION AND THE MOAT

So far, we've gotten to a point where we are comfortable talking about industries and the companies within them as potential areas for investigation. We've established where we have an interest and started to build mental maps of supplier relationships with companies.

Now, we are getting to the most crucial understanding I think one can have about an investment: the competitive landscape. Buffett talks about moats. Some companies have very deep ones, established over the years, with crocodiles in them and armies to defend them.

In my view, the ability to contemplate competition and understand what could potentially undermine a business is not merely crucial; it is the pivotal aspect of capitalism. Companies are established to solve a need the consumer has, or else the consumer won't pay for it.

It's Christmastime as I write this, and if you don't believe that companies are set up to take money from consumers, go visit your local mall.

About malls. I find walking through malls to be extremely necessary for the job of a portfolio manager. The year before I was born, the Staten Island Mall opened just a couple miles from my house. A trip to that mall was the highlight of the week for me and my family. At one end of the mall stood an anchor: Macy's—still in existence and renowned for the parade that bears its name. However, over the years, the department store business has faced extraordinary challenges. What makes me say that? At the other end, the anchor tenant was Sears.

In 1974, a year after the Staten Island Mall opened, the Sears Tower, the 110-story tallest building in the world, opened. 44 years later, Sears would file for bankruptcy. When you walk across a shopping mall, ask yourself if ANY of these brands could build the tallest building in the world for its headquarters (it's now the Willis Tower). Sears later merged with a discount leader – Kmart, which was once larger than Walmart and ended up bankrupt 44 years after building the tower. That's what happens.

By the way, it's sometimes a good mind exercise to think about companies and even societies building skyscrapers as a prelude to something bad. If you reallocate your capital into a skyscraper, is that a smart investment move or a sign of hubris?

Do we consume less as a nation? No way. Do we need Sears? Obviously not. Or its once ubiquitous competitor, JCPenney. Incidentally, we had an outdoor shopping center only a few miles from the Staten Island mall that was anchored by a JCPenney and a Kmart.

NONE of these stores would have been pegged—by the consumer—for bankruptcy. Who builds a 110-story building when planning for bankruptcy?

Not people who had this and basically everything any family could want to buy in their 1974 Wish Book.

Note the fact that $21.78 wouldn't get you the wheels on that wagon (it's $108 on Amazon).

What moats did they have? Sears had 3500 stores at its peak. This Wish Book catalog was THE book

I—and most of my friends—used to guide Santa Claus. That book was the descendant of the first catalogs launched in 1892 when Sears came into business.

A trip to the mall would bring you past Radio Shack. There were 7000 of those in the nation at the peak, back in 20003. Tell high school-aged me that they'd effectively be gone (along with Sears), and I would have argued vehemently about that. Again, list some brands you see today that you couldn't fathom being bankrupt.

It's not all bad news. Not too far away was one of the newer additions to Staten Island, a McDonalds. They've done fine.

We didn't go there, though, because my grandmother wanted us to eat higher quality food and also didn't like the "misbehaved kids" who were at McDonald's. We went to the Bun N' Burger, which was a staple in malls in the region, home of massive burgers, steak fries and incredible cheese sauce. Sadly, they are gone. McDonald's, on the other hand, dominates.

CREATIVE DESTRUCTION—JOSEPH SCHUMPETER, ANOTHER HERO

My mentor in the business, Rick, told me about "Creative Destruction" and Schumpeter when I was first looking at imaging technology stocks back in 2000. It is one of THE major lessons of my early career (along with his insistence I finish the CFA—thanks, Rick!) We'll cover imaging technology later and why there's often a right and DEAD wrong time to buy stocks that are in hot industries.

The essence of this is that innovation ultimately drives us forward but, at the same time, necessitates the destruction of prior realities. For instance, this is being written on a Mac laptop that effectively destroys the typewriter I'd have written it on 50-60 years ago. The poor guy who used to clean horse crap off of fifth avenue saw his job destroyed when trollies came into being, and later those trolly tracks were ripped out to make way for the cars that jam Fifth Avenue.

Schumpeter, the originator of Creative Destruction, went so far as to say that Creative Destruction is an essential fact about capitalism."

Consider Schumpeter is at your side when you plan your investment—"Economic progress, in a capitalist society, means turmoil."

Make yourself a Schumpeter checklist when you shop. Can this business be replaced? Do you need it? How can it be replaced by other companies, products, and services? This is what Jeff Bezos did. This is how Steve Jobs behaved. They are not just destroying (as people say). They are creating. Consider the world before Amazon? Or WalMart. Actually, go back in time and consider before Mr Sears came up with his catalog. Yes, people lost businesses and jobs. By the way, think about how many businesses have been replaced by Home Depot – the local hardware guy had to innovate or be destroyed. However, so too did the second-rate competitors like Pergament, Channel, Rickel, etc. Sam Walton was credited with the idea "stack 'em high and let 'em fly" in terms of mass retailing. Anyone could have done the same, but THEY CHOSE NOT TO. Same with Costco. It's deflationary. People win with it.

Porter. The Five Forces

Like Schumpeter, Professor Michael E. Porter from the Harvard Business School was highlighted to me by my mentor and also in the CFA program at that point (early 2000s). Porter laid out the "Five Competitive Forces."

These two frameworks, Creative Destruction and The Five Forces, form a great reference to analyze

1. Threat of New Entrants
2. Bargaining Power of Suppliers
3. Bargaining Power of Buyers
4. Threat of Substitute Products or Services
5. Rivalry Among Existing Competitors

Note our friends in the department store category suffered from 1-big time. Notice how I went to Amazon to figure out what that wagon costs. Point 5 was also a major piece. It would be difficult to imagine suppliers telling Sears to go to hell in 1974. That dramatically changed as people got choices. Hang up Porter's Five Forces in your room along with a photo of Schumpeter when you think your business is unassailable.

One of the best kinds of business analogies – and you know I love analogies—comes from the razor, razor blade concept that originated with King Gillette (best founder name) and is a safety razor. Gillette solved something mundane and created not only a brand that is now part of Berkshire Hathaway. Thanks to his acquisition, Buffett ensures that we shareholders get a piece of the inevitable growth of unwanted body hair.

Could Gilette be unseated by new entrants? Sure—there have recently been a raft of competing products for men and women, including subscription and internet products.

While in engineering school, I took an exceptional course—the only undergraduate-level business course I ever attended—Engineering Management with Professor Robert Barrett. The course was—and is—all I needed because it formalized my understanding of how companies are led, the different management styles and the concept of "plan, organize, staff, direct, control." Professor Barrett's course solidified my already keen desire to get out of Cooper, eschew engineering and go back to Wall Street as an analyst. Thanks, Professor (by the way, my best buddies from Cooper, with whom I talk every day, also have very fond memories of his class).

Anyway, one of the razor-blade businesses I wrote about in an assignment related to Total Quality Management was the then-mighty Hewlett-Packard printer of the mid-1990s. To me, it represented one of the perfect products—tremendous brand loyalty among knowledgeable people (engineering students) and high-margin blade—laser and print cartridges that had us all spending each time we printed.

HP still has a 1/3 share of the market for printers (though that is down over 10 percentage points since just 18 years ago). That share has gone somewhere. And that is what Porter and Schumpeter are about.

Armed with these two heroes in mind, I would encourage you to think about these companies.

Make a “mental map”. Spend 10-15 minutes thinking and listing the companies that would want to destroy, I mean absolutely obliterate these competitors. I want you to consider the management teams whose obsession it is to destroy these companies, to replace them.

McDonald's has Wendy’s, Burger King, Popeyes, and Subway. They’re all competing for “share of a belly." Coke has its Pepsi. Starbucks has Dunkin Donuts. Apple has had IBM, Dell, Microsoft (which also helped in the late 1990s to resurrect them) Nokia, Ericsson, Google, Nvidia has Intel and AMD. Telsa has GM, Ford, Toyota, Honda, BMW, Daimler, BYD.

You could actually go back to the Yahoo finance screener to get a good picture of whether or not they’re publicly traded or even get started there.

Sure, these companies would love, Tony Montana style, to go and metaphorically, of course, shoot up their competitors and the various threats to their business. That’s management’s job!

SAY HELLO TO MY LITTLE FRIEND

Of course, back in the old days when I was a young apprentice analyst, the only way to get good competitive data was 1) to go through the 10Ks of the target company, look for the names, then go to THEIR 10Ks and see if they corresponded and to look at THEIR competitors as well 2) go to the internet, albeit a much slower, much less comprehensive one in the late 90s than it is today, 3) go to the one Bloomberg terminal on the floor, which was then (and is now) a $2000+ per month device.

Today, for the purposes of basic research, you now have a "little friend" known as ChatGPT. I asked it to list the top 10 competitors for McDonald's (MCD) with their ticker symbols, if relevant, and their rough revenue. No surprises here.

ChatGPT 4

1. **Starbucks** (SBUX): Approximately $30 billion. Starbucks is a global leader in the coffee segment and is publicly traded.
2. **Subway**: Around $10 billion. Subway is a privately-held company and does not have a ticker symbol.
3. **Yum! Brands** (YUM): Roughly $30 billion combined. Yum! Brands, the parent company of KFC, Pizza Hut, and Taco Bell, is publicly traded.
4. **Burger King**: Part of Restaurant Brands International (QSR), with an estimated revenue of $20 billion. Burger King is under the umbrella of Restaurant Brands International, which is a publicly traded company.
5. **Wendy's** (WEN): About $12 billion. Wendy's is a publicly traded company known for its hamburgers and fast-food offerings.
6. **Domino's Pizza** (DPZ): Approximately $15 billion. Domino's, a leader in the pizza delivery segment, is publicly traded.
7. **Dunkin' (Dunkin' Donuts)**: Previously traded as DNKN. Dunkin' was taken private in late 2020 by Inspire Brands and no longer has a ticker symbol.
8. **Chick-fil-A**: Estimated $16 billion. Chick-fil-A is a privately-held company and does not have a ticker symbol.
9. **Chipotle Mexican Grill** (CMG): Roughly $8 billion. Chipotle, specializing in Mexican cuisine, is a publicly traded company.
10. **Sonic Drive-In**: Part of Inspire Brands, with about $5 billion in revenue. Sonic was previously publicly traded as SONC but i ↓ w privately owned under Inspire Brands.

Here's what ChatGPT 4 outputs for Tesla

ChatGPT 4

1. **Toyota Motor Corporation** (TM): Toyota, known for its hybrid technology and increasingly for its EV developments, has significant revenue, approximately $275 billion.
2. **Volkswagen AG** (VWAGY): Volkswagen, actively investing in EV technology, has revenues around $280 billion.
3. **General Motors** (GM): GM, with its commitment to an all-electric future, generates revenues of about $127 billion.
4. **Ford Motor Company** (F): Ford, entering the EV market with models like the Mustang Mach-E and the electric F-150, has revenues around $136 billion.
5. **BMW Group** (BMW.DE): BMW, with its luxury electric vehicles, reports revenues of approximately $116 billion.
6. **Daimler AG** (DAI.DE): Daimler, the parent company of Mercedes-Benz, known for its luxury EVs, has revenues of about $193 billion.
7. **Nissan Motor Co., Ltd.** (NSANY): Nissan, with its popular Leaf EV model, has revenues around $80 billion.
8. **Hyundai Motor Company** (HYMTF): Hyundai, increasingly focusing on EVs, reports revenues of approximately $90 billion.
9. **Stellantis N.V.** (STLA): Formed from the merger of Fiat Chrysler Automobiles and PSA Group, Stellantis is expanding its EV lineup, with revenues of around $150 billion.
10. **NIO Inc.** (NIO): NIO, a Chinese EV manufa ↓ er specializing in smart, high-performance electric vehicles, has revenues of about $5 billion.

I am increasingly using ChatGPT as a "junior analyst" and recommend you should, too. It is like having an electric motor to get you out on a lake to the bigger fish—it is NOT a substitute (yet, or maybe ever?) for a true fishing guide or junior analyst. It is perfect for this type of basic research.

Later, we are going to go into how to read 10-Ks (annual reports), and I'll show you how to expand this list the old-fashioned way.

Imaging, Kodak Xerox, Polaroid, Nifty Fifty

Another word about destruction. Do not think it is inapplicable. I came into the industry in the late 1990s with digital imaging still a concept and flat panel TVs not yet ubiquitous. In the year 2000, Eastman Kodak was THE dominant player in photography, which—at that point, was Silver Halide photography. They had invented digital photography in the 1970s! But, it's now 2024 and they are interestingly ancient history. Remember Polaroid? They, along with Kodak, were in some sense the Apple of their day (back in the 1970s) both in terms of consumer reach AND in terms of multiples. 24 years ago, they still had a business of selling photography to consumers and professionals. Today, good luck finding people shooting with film.

So what can we do about this?

The world of paired training, hedging, and even statistical arbitrage will be opened to you later in the book, and you'll need more than this book to get good at these. Suffice it to say that there are industry-specific problems that plague ALL of the companies within your favorite's chosen sector. There's also a winner-take-all element to some industries. Wouldn't it be cool to insure against all of the above?

We will discuss all of this later, because when you see that there is a change coming, such as the demise of film, or the rise of some technology that will creatively destroy your business, you can hedge, you can do pairs trading, and you can protect and even benefit from calamity.

I was born in the 1970s and was shaped by a lot of the 1970s and 1980s TV—I gave up TV in the early 1990s thanks to my renegade and legendary AP English Teacher. Junk Dealers like Sanford and Son resonate with me, because Fred and Lamont were able to make a living and have a nice little house finding and reselling things people had discarded. In some respects, you can do this with fallen companies like the aforementioned film companies. Beware, though, because often the low multiples mask problems that are ALREADY identified.

CHAPTER 7
PE, RELATIVE VALUATION ASSET VALUATION SCREENING

Everything has led to this: Valuation.

Thank you for sticking with me. You have demonstrated temperament, and you have developed, with me, some new frameworks for looking at stocks and the underlying businesses. You understand and endorse the concept that they are not just pieces of paper or "trading sardines" but fractional pieces of business. Most importantly, you know how to rule out areas where you don't have—or can't establish—some edge. You've built a funnel to narrow down your universe.

Valuation:

It is the most important element of investing. There is NOTHING more important. You can quote me. And if you disagree, please email me/call me, and we can have a debate on it. I'm ready. brian@broadwaycap.com. Email me ESPECIALLY if you think valuation doesn't matter.

All elements of your buy or sell thesis are contingent upon asking the crucial question, "What is this worth?" and then determining if the stock price departs widely enough from that to offer a margin of safety. If the stock is worth $10 and the market is selling it to you for $10, it's not a buy. But if it's trading at $5?!? Probably, if you've done your work.

The market is wrong all the time. Repeat this often. Your job from now on is to figure out what the thing is worth and if the market is wrong. That's the job. If the stock is worth $10 and the market is paying $100 for it, there's additional nuance to shorting (you don't just go and short it, you do nothing or buy puts but we'll talk about that later).

Remember, there are "no called strikes," as Buffett has noted. You can look at 100s of stocks trading close to what you determine to be fair value and just wait for the market to throw it your way at an appropriate discount. And there is NO penalty. You are looking for asymmetric returns, and those don't come with every "pitch".

Some basic terminology you should know at this point. We already discussed market capitalization, which is the total equity capital in the company. Enterprise value takes into account all forms of capital in the company (both equity AND debt) and effectively is Equity (common plus preferred) plus net debt (total debt less cash).

The market price tells you a lot about what people will sell you the stock for and simultaneously tells you nothing about the value of the business. "Price is what you pay, value is what you get", as Buffett has said.

It's a bit more than that-what does the price actually "tell you." The only way to get at that is to invert, as Munger said, quoting the alebraist Jacobi, who said **"man muss immer umkehren" according to James Clear (https: // jamesclear. Com**

/inversion). Price is exactly what the market says the business is worth, but what is the "intrinsic value"?

This has been a significant debate throughout my career, originating with proponents of the efficient market hypothesis. I am watching a stock trade up 449% today. Yesterday's price was fair, and today's price is fair, per the EMH guys, to simplify. Over the years, I've met people who said value doesn't matter. Value is what it is. I'd be worried about buying something for which I have no idea what the value is. In fact, it would be like walking onto an unlit highway like the old Frogger video game. Fortunately, there are guideposts and lights all over the place.

AND WE know better. We're in on the secret (to many, it seems) that you're actualy buying a business when you're buying a stock.

And, as long as there are people trading momentum and technical stuff and treating stocks like pieces of paper, I'm happy because there's a chance they're not doing the work, not considering intrinsic value, not paying attention to what really matters and thus liable to trade based on emotion, charts, daily noise/news, chairman Powell, etc. I'll buy from them and sell to them for the rest of my career.

Triangulation

I'll give you a secret right now, so you don't need to read ahead. The BEST valuation method, the one I find to be most rigorous and consistent with the way capital is allocated within the business, is the discounted free cash flow to the equity method. Cash is king. This method recognizes that.

We'll talk more about that later because you need to build up to it—you'll need some toolkit that I promise to provide you (and that your second-grade math teacher already gave you a lot of).

Let's go back to Yahoo Finance's screener.

In the United States, there are 98 publicly traded restaurants, ranging in size from McDonald's to Gourmet Provisions. Yahoo Finance gives a PE ratio for each of the profitable ones.

This is the most basic ratio. The market capitalization is divided by the GAAP (generally accepted accounting principles) earnings. The higher the PE, the more "expensive" the stock is on earnings. The PE is just a snapshot. It tells you nothing other than in a relative way.

Relative to what? Cross-sectionally: To other companies within the segment and to the general market. Temporally—to the past and the future. These are clues to what market participants think about the company itself versus other companies and the future.

Ok, so McDonalds trades at 25x. Years back, an institutional salesman, looking at a "high" PE relative to others, said, "That means it'll take me 25 years to get my money back. That's partly true, and it's not necessarily a dumb way to look at the SHORTHAND that is "PE." Partly true because McDonald's will most likely grow its earnings (more hungry people born by the day, more net restaurants being opened annually, possible operating leverage, meaning incremental revenue growth of a certain percentage will translate into incremental earnings growth. So, it'll take 25 years if current earnings are stagnant.

What does a 25 PE mean? Invert it in your mind for a minute. That's a 4% earnings yield. Keep this in mind for later analysis.

Look at it versus the other participants in the group. Direct competitor Wendy's trades at 20x. Chipotle trades at DOUBLE the multiple, 54x. Cheesecake factory trades at 14x. Shake Shack sports a 259 multiple of earnings!

Buying low PE stocks merely because they are low relative PE stocks can spell disaster, however. For one, everyone is looking at these same sets of numbers. Heck, you can look at them for FREE! Is Wendy's "worth" a 20% discount to McDonald's? Perhaps. Is Shake Shack "worth" 10x what McDonalds is on current earnings? I don't have enough information. If PE were the ONLY indicator available to us, and all stocks' mean reverted to some mean PE, we would short Shake Shack and buy McDonald's. It's not that easy AT ALL (but you're on the right track toward triangulating things).

We're going to depart our trusted friend Yahoo Finance to another—even more comprehensive, but still free(!) stock screener brought to us by Zacks.

With Zacks, we have access to more screening criteria than Yahoo provides. I would still use Yahoo for initial screening because it tends to pick up a wider range of market caps. However, in Zacks, we get much more screening tools.

In the restaurant group, we go with Zacks.

We are still in the relative value game, just checking a group of related companies to define valuation characteristics. However, we now have two additional pieces: an estimate of earnings growth (implied by the forward year PE) and Price/Sales.

Let's screen not only for trailing PE but also for the estimated PE, and let's also screen for P/S. We see that the median price to sales is 1.3x, with a range of 0.19 (Meritage, MHGU) to Wingstop (17.1x). Meritage is a franchisee of Wendy's, with 382 restaurants, per its 2023 CEO report. Wingstop is a franchisor of chicken restaurants, with 1950 locations worldwide, per its 2022 annual report. Both restaurants are businesses in quick service, but they have different business models. Note that McDonald's has the second-highest P/S ratio of 8.4x

Later, we'll talk about unit sales and valuation per unit, and since these two live at extreme valuations, we'll stick with them.

Zacks gives us the ability to look at forward-year PE, as well as the trailing, to get a sense of implied growth.

Sorted this way, the lowest PE is Dine Brands (DINE). Dine owns two famous casual restaurants: Applebees and IHOP, originally known as the International House of Pancakes (my incredible wife still lets me take her there). According to the screen, Dine trades at a trailing PE of 7.47x and a forward

PE of 7.69x—the "street" effectively targets flat earnings growth.

Who, you say, is the Street? They are a collection of analysts employed by brokerage firms to come up with earnings forecasts that feed into this type of service (Yahoo Finance, Zacks, and the pay-for-play Bloomberg, etc). A lot of us started careers as these types of analysts, known as "Sell Side" analysts because ultimately, they are selling ideas and generating commissions (and, at one time, corporate finance/investment banking business) for these firms.

They, like you, are people. They get up in the morning, spill coffee, fight with their spouses, make mistakes in spreadsheets. Some are amazing at ferreting out company data; some are good at getting management meetings; some are semi-retired and managing a team of 25 year olds who concoct the estimates. None are superhuman (though I know quite a few who are fantastic at what they do). The average estimate is a collection of people making a judgment the same way you and I do. They are handicapping next year's numbers based on the models they build. I've viewed them as useful insofar as it's a division of labor—most of them specialize in a specific industry (such as fast food restaurants) and thus are spending the majority of their time on something. Their numbers aren't always right, and their recommendations about whether a stock is a buy/sell/hold are not something upon which you can bet your financial future—the "skin in the game" is often missing. You don't have access to them, to get the appropriate caveats in their models, the ranges of possibilities they've thought about in coming up with ther estimates. It actually doesn't really matter. I digress again, and we'll spend a lot more time speaking about what IS important (earnings power) versus what is not (point estimates, precisely wrong) for investing. Buffett has talked about being "roughly right," and that's what I encourage because focusing too much on what a company will earn down to the penny for the next 90 days misses the point, involves too much unnecessary labor (and trading based on it can be filled with peril).

I like to look at the average as well as the max and min to get an idea of the range within the group. Do not mistake a higher-than-average multiple for something that is "too expensive" or a lower-than-average multiple for something that is "too cheap." Further investigation into why a higher or lower multiple is required, and that comes from looking not only at the financials—we'll do that in another chapter—but also understanding sentiment around the business, for instance, the perception of growth opportunity (or lack thereof). This CAN be a quantitative game, wholly—in fact, heroes of the industry like Dr. Thorp or Dr. Simons have made fortunes doing quantitative. Relative PE is not enough.

Let's stay looking at relative earnings-related measures for a minute. We've explored the multiple of sales.

EV/EBITDA? What is that? Is EBITDA bullshit, as Munger said?

Another shorthand valuation measure people use is EV/EBITDA. EV, as we discussed, is Enterprise Value—the total amount of capitalization according to the company—Equity (both common and preferred) plus Debt minus cash. Think of it this way: if you wanted to bid for a company, you'd make a bid for the equity (to buy out the owners), but you'd also have to take on the debt that was used to finance the company. Debt is not necessarily an evil thing since it is often MUCH cheaper than issuing shares—so don't eschew companies that have it. Mature businesses should be able to finance their business using the bond market or banks—it is not necessarily the same as personal finance.

EBITDA stands for Earnings Before Interest Tax Depreciation and Amortization. Effectively, looking from the Revenue line down, it's earnings available to service interest, taxes, depreciation and amortization.

The argument for using this is that EBITDA can mimic cash flow (that can be true, but only SOMEtimes) and normalizes companies within an industry, making them agnostic to capital structure.

The problem comes from stopping analysis at that level because CFOs and accountants can move around (legally) depreciation and amortization, and both taxes and interest can also move around from year to year. To say one company has an EV/EBITDA of 4 versus another one at 6 doesn't say much if a company at 4 has been starving its investment in plant and equipment (depreciation is very low on old stuff) or 6 decided to expense a lot of R&D rather than capitalize and depreciate it.

Let's address Munger's claim that EBITDA is "bullshit." As with a lot of shorthand invented by investment bankers, it has a high degree of that, with an innocent enough genesis (they wanted to normalize among capital-intensive telecommunications companies). The problem arose when analysts began stopping their analysis of it. And forgetting that D&A can be real numbers—real cash out the door. A lot of money can be made on Wall Street because people are in a hurry to come to a conclusion and/or sell you something. Free cash flow is the ultimate arbiter of a business—EBITDA is not free cash flow. I worked with a veteran institutional investor who, in the aftermath of the 2000 tech meltdown, told me, "I KNEW those f'ing EBITDA companies were crap."

Zacks does not have EV/EBITDA available in its free version anyway, which is fine by me because I prefer to look at cash flow. They evidently do, too.

After looking at each of these valuation multiples, I want to remind you that this is all shorthand. The fair value is the net present value of all the cash the business will generate. P/E only tells part of the story, as does P/S.

I know—I have told you that shortcuts are important. However...

Cash is king. So, we need to get at the free cash flow to equity model.

A quick aside is the Magic Formula book written by Joel Greenblatt, famous for his 50% cagr over his first decade, his adherence to value principles and his teaching at Columbia's Business School. He ties together two crucial things: a multiple (EV/EBIT—not EBITDA) and Return on Invested Capital. We'll cover return characteristics later, but they are very important.

The magic formula is combining low EV/EBIT (statistical "cheapness") with high ROIC—management's ability to translate corporate activity into good payback on capital put into the business.

What is ROIC? It is NOPAT/Invested Capital. What is NOPAT? Net operating profit after taxes. Earnings before Interest and Taxes MINUS Cash Taxes.

What is invested capital?

(Short Term Debt+Long Term Debt+Deferred Taxes+Other Liabilities+Preferred Stock+Common Equity)

Here's a great primer on NOPAT:

https://www.morganstanley.com/im/publication/insights/articles/article_returnoninvestedcapital.pdf

These definitions come from the work of Michael Mauboussin, who, along with Professor Aswath Damodaran are titans of valuation, and both introduced to me by my mentor Rick.

Professor Greenblatt tied together elements of what I've been talking about in such an elegant way we could probably stop here. In some senses, this is like the Maxwell's equations I learned about in engineering school that tie together electricity and magnetism.

With his work, you can rank order companies based on the combination (you invert EV/EBIT so you get an "earnings yield" and then multiply that by the ROIC, so the higher the number, the more desirable the company.)

We're getting toward a better way to compare and contrast companies. As with engineering a building or a road, you need a datum, a point of reference, around which the thing can be built.

So, at this point, you can triangulate PE, forward PE, and Price to Sales and have a glimpse into the Magic Formula.

Here are another bunch of considerations:

Asset valuation

At the core of many businesses lies a literal goldmine worth of value. Mining companies have reserves that certainly do lend themselves to NPV (net present value) calculations like the discounted cash flow model we'll discuss, but you can also model out the actual metal in the ground based on reserve reports and come up with a shorthand value of the company making an assumption about the metal price, the cost to extract the metal and the time to deplete the mine.

This also works for companies like oil and E&Ps, but also for real estate, in which you can look at the replacement value of the building or even land values.

Later, we'll talk about the sum of the parts as well, in which you can take an asset valuation and combine that with an earnings-driven valuation. For instance, looking at fast food businesses broken up into the operating companies, the franchise model, and the land was how I got introduced by Bill Ackman's work to this framework on McDonalds.

Ben Graham used to find net/nets companies trading at a discount to net working capital. These occasionally come up, but remember, people have been following him for 90 years!

Remember, there's franchise value, the intangible stuff that has LOTS of value, like brands, customer lists, and expensed R&D and moats.

What about intangible assets such as brands, patents, etc?

R&D can be capitalized—look at past expensed R&D. I learned this lesson talking to one of Ben Graham's early disciples, the late Mr. Irving Kahn

Sales and Marketing build brands. What is the BRAND worth?

Maybe there are NO tangible assets. Is it worthless? Clearly, something makes money, and that's intellectual property.

Buying a business is ALWAYS about what kind of cash it can produce, either to reinvest in things that earn above its "cost of capital."

But what do you think about free cash flow?

The next chapter ties it all together!

Meanwhile, if you have ANY questions, let's get together. Contact me at brian@broadwaycap.com

www.convexityhunter.com

CHAPTER 8
FREE CASH FLOW TO EQUITY. THE QUEEN OF ALL MODELS

We have come far, establishing our comfort with screening and picking the basic multiples, such as PE (both past and forward), Price to Sales and EV/EBIT. We've discussed the shortcomings of each and the concept that for a "quick and dirty" view of how the market views a business, they are good shorthand, nevertheless. We've delved into uniting EV/EBIT with return on invested capital, as Professor Joel Greenblatt shows us how to do.

We're well along on our journey. However, as Yoda says in Return of the Jedi, "incomplete was your training. Not ready for the burden, were you."

Sure, you can go out with what you've established in the first seven chapters and do a decent job building a portfolio. Heck, I believe that most professional investors rely on just a few tools, and—indeed—one of the greatest of all time published the Magic Formula. You can absolutely build a good portfolio based on that website, in my humble opinion. There are "set it and forget it" rules out there.

However—to become a great investor, you must face Darth Vader!

I'm kidding. I think to become a great investor, you must understand discounted cash flow analysis.

In order to do that, you have to understand cash flow. This is superior to GAAP earnings because cash flow, specifically FREE cash flow, is the actual cash left over in a business after all expenses, working capital movements and capital expenditures are made. It's the true earnings power of a business, and it's really the way you'd think about profits in a private business. Imagine a simple business making burgers. The income statement would report a topline (revenue) consisting of burger sales. You'd have short-term cash expenses such as inventory (meat, buns, cheese), salaries, rent, sales, marketing, interest on loans and—if the revenue less the "accrued" expenses meant a profit, taxes.

Accrual accounting is different from cash accounting—it is NOT inferior, it is only different. Suppose you buy equipment for making these burgers. That equipment involves possibly a large capital expense upfront. It's silly to expense the whole thing, an asset with perhaps 10 or more years of burger making abilities in year one, even if the cash goes out the door on day 1. You either finance that with debt or pay with cash, but the actual use of that long-term capital asset (let's say a fryer) comprises more than just the year in which it is bought. Accountants have, at their discretion, rules (generally accepted accounting principles) for allocating the economic cost of that asset to appropriate periods. In other words, across the life of the equipment, the cost is allocated to the burger sales. As an analyst, you want to figure out the maintenance cash flow per unit (per burger may be too precise, but per year is doable, and should reflect the wear and tear you see on the equipment—get it?)

Sometimes, accelerated depreciation is permitted—you make the expenditure for the equipment, and the depreciation is taken earlier than the actual device is used. This can be done to decrease reported earnings to the tax authorities.

In capital-intensive businesses, it makes sense to understand the REAL life versus the GAAP accounting (accrual) life of the asset so you can understand what maintenance capital expenditures are. A 30-year life piece of equipment may be depreciated in much shorter periods, for instance, as permitted by GAAP and the tax code.

In some cases, GAAP earnings understate the true economic reality of a business because R&D and marketing expenses are expensed as incurred. You're building intellectual property that will CERTAINLY generate returns, but those dollars are being expensed through the income statement. You're building a brand, another type of moat that is expensed through SG&A.

Later, we'll deconstruct the cash flow statement, but my advice is to look at the Operating Cash Flow before you look at earnings.

Free cash flow is simply Operating Cash Flow less maintenance Capital Expenditures. For maintenance, your job is to make the appropriate adjustment. Say an airline with $20 million in operating cash buys a $100 million jet with a 10-year life. That $100 million is run through the first-year cash flow statement. OCF-CAPEX is $80 million for that year, but more realistically, it's closer to $10 million (20 million less 100/10).

The hero of this chapter is John Burr Williams, who, in 1938, released the Theory of Investment Value (TOIV), a book recommended to me by an early (and unfortunately gone too early) mentor, Tony Russ, who was a partner of Rick, my primary mentor.

In TOIV, Williams introduced the concept of Discounted Cash Flow models as the main way to value equity securities. Bond investors do this math all the time—it's not difficult. DCF ties together the discipline of understanding the earnings power of a company over time (which is what you should do if you're buying into a business) with the future cash flows discounted due to the cost of equity, which itself can be broken into two additive factors: 1) the "risk-free rate"—basically the prevailing long term rate on treasuries, because a buck today is worth less than a buck in the future, and a buck lent to the "full faith and credit" will be worth 1+(risk-free rate) in a year. 2) some kind of "Equity Risk Premium."

There are two pieces here that are subject to YOUR discretion. The numerators are your estimates of the annual free cash flow generated by the company. These estimates come from all your biases –they have to (and don't kid yourself that there is precision), as well as the empirical data you've collected.

The first year is the easy part—you can get year 1 from the 10-K or Zacks. That's Operating Cash Flow less Capex (maintenance). OCF is right there for you.

Over a series of years, you can get a good idea of what kind of cash the company generates by looking through the public filings—we'll spend more time later on how to do this.

McDonald's does a good job of discussing cash flow.

CASH FLOWS

The Company has a long history of generating significant cash from operations and has substantial credit capacity to fund operating and discretionary spending such as capital expenditures, debt repayments, dividends and share repurchases.

Cash provided by operations totaled $7.4 billion in 2022, a decrease of $1.7 billion or 19%. Free cash flow was $5.5 billion in 2022, a decrease of $1.6 billion or 23%. The Company's free cash flow conversion rate was 89% in 2022 and 94% in 2021. Cash provided by operations decreased in 2022 compared to 2021 primarily due to the settlement of a tax audit in France, changes in working capital, and the negative impact of foreign currency rates on operating results.

Cash used for investing activities totaled $2.7 billion in 2022, an increase of $512 million compared with 2021. The increase was primarily due to higher purchases of restaurant businesses, partly offset by proceeds from the sale of Dynamic Yield in 2022 and proceeds from the sale of McDonald's Japan stock in 2021.

Cash used for financing activities totaled $6.6 billion in 2022, an increase of $1.0 billion compared with 2021. The increase was primarily due to increased treasury stock purchases, partly offset by increased net debt issuances.

The Company's cash and equivalents balance was $2.6 billion and $4.7 billion at year end 2022 and 2021, respectively. In addition to cash and equivalents on hand and cash provided by operations, the Company can meet short-term funding needs throug its continued access to commercial paper borrowings and line of credit agreements.

The secret ingredients to constructing a free cash flow model are, 1) build the cash flow model for the next 5-10 years or split it into supernormal growth and a stable GDP-like growth period, 2) consider an appropriate discount rate.

A LOT of assumptions go into this that some consider arbitrary and are a major criticism of the model.

1) How can you reasonably determine future growth (good question, we'll get to that)?
2) How can you be sure the discount rate is "right" (also a super question)?
3) How can you figure out at what point the supernormal growth period stops and the "terminal value" (the value at which growth is stable and GDP-like) ?

Each of these questions has an answer grounded in heuristics—rules of thumb. And like PE, P/S, EV/EBIT, this is just one more TOOL. Can you build a house with just a screwdriver? Sure. I view the free cash flow model as a Swiss Army Knife on steroids.

It has a bunch of different elements to it that you SHOULD want to think about when owning a business—it enables you to think about the earnings varability of the business as well as the financing of it, PLUS forces you to think about risk through the deployment of a discount/hurdle rate. You're going to be roughly right on each of the elements, NOT precise. But that's also true with all the other simpler multiples.

Build the model! But how???

For easy companies that have one product, building a workable financial model driven by key assumptions isn't very difficult. You need Excel (or its equivalent) and access to the company's 10-ks and Qs.

You can start with the topline revenue and think about what the next 3,5,10 years would look like for revenue growth. Is the company part of a cycle (like CAT tractors)? Is it pretty steady in terms of demand growth (like hamburgers) but with nascent competition? Are they in a mature market (autos) but building something that is penetrating market share within that market (like Tesla)? The TYPE of company and TYPE of industry, along with the moat, the competition and—yes—macro factors, will play a role in what your topline growth looks like.

What about gross margins? Here, you have to think about the cost of goods (burger meat, cola syrup, equipment depreciation) and have a gut (HA) feeling about what it takes to grow.

Does the company possess operating leverage? In other words, for each percent increase in sales, do the earnings grow more quickly?

If a lot of this sounds like extrapolating recent history, basically looking at x% growth and plugging in (1+x%)*the column immediately to the left, it can be that simple.

Another way:

Consider the company's past return on invested capital (ROIC) as a guide for how it can grow earnings. If an industry has a 10% ROIC, with a range of 0-15%, it may be silly to think of 30% ROIC in your model.

Remember, unlike the security analysts you see on television or whose EPS estimates you see as averaged into "the consensus," you can have a few models, a small/medium/large scenario analysis that includes what happens if the economy is soft, competition is intense on one and what happens if there are tailwinds on the other end.

So you will be 3x as good as the typical Wall Street analyst because you will have THREE models. Actually it's better than that, because there is synergistic goodness.

See how long you can reasonably extrapolate this into the future without the thing being bigger than the entire economy—I'm not kidding here. Some people have said implicitly that a company making cars can grow to be 20% of the entire US economy. Think in terms of addressable markets when you're building your growth model. Think in terms of what it will take (there are only 3 meals in a day, and there are limits on how many cans of beer an individual can consume, how many cars they can drive, and how many laptops per home).

It may be absurd to think of a large company in a mature market growing revenues 15% per year for the next 5 years, for instance—that implies that coming into the sixth year, you'll have doubled revenues. Can the business you're analyzing do that? Think of a restaurant chain. If it's $100 million in sales, it is entirely possible to become a $200 million thing. It becomes a lot harder to do if it does $25 billion in sales, the way McDonald's does, or $66 billion in sales, the way Anheuser-Busch InBev does.

Can earnings increase at 15% on a 5% revenue growth company? Absolutely, and they do because of operating leverage.

Remember, we're drilling down into a model of free cash flow. Cash revenue less cash expenses and working capital changes effectively get us to operating cash flow. Remember, operating cash flow is NOT EBITDA. Cash interest and cash taxes do figure into cash flow (the cash really goes out the door to bondholders, lenders, and governments). Depreciation accrual concepts discussed before actually DO NOT have a direct cash impact on cash flow but do represent an estimation of cash outlays that will be in capex.

Over time, you should look at the percentage growth of line items as well as the percentage of revenues for these line items—you can compare them to other companies in the sector, for instance, common size.

Modeling maintenance capex comes down to understanding the plant and equipment in the business. An airline is capital intensive, and a restaurant is too—and not just for equipment, but also for keeping the restaurants looking fresh. Brewing equipment needs to be maintained.

Think of maintenance capex as both a percent of sales and a percent of the existing property plant and equipment you'll see on the balance sheet. Over time, the percentages remain somewhat fixed. Too much deviation one way or the other should prompt questions. And it's not a bad thing, necessarily, if the company buys new equipment, but you don't want to take that big growth in capex as a permanent thing necessarily.

Once you've come up with a good estimate of OCF and maintenance capex, you have an idea of FREE CASH FLOW.

Free cash flow would be, for the owner of a private business, the most important thing to think about because when you own a private business, your local tailor, your grocery store, or your kid's college tuition, you take free cash flow in return for what they provide you. I can't go to a fancy restaurant with a wad full of EBITDA.

Discount Rate?

The rationale behind the discount rate is that a dollar today is worth more than a dollar in the future. The most basic discount rate is a real one, inflation—

the government says that its target for your dollar's purchasing power is being destroyed at a rate of 2-3% per year. The government borrows from you "risk-free" at some rate above that, say 4-5% (though as low as 0). You can lend money to the government and effectively get 2-3% above inflation without the risk of default.

Stocks are riskier than that. So are your assumptions about the earnings. One way John Burr Williams thought about this is that you would DEMAND a higher rate than the risk-free rate or any bond rate for going into equities.

How much? For corporate bonds, there should be some kind of spread—they can default and can't print their way out of it. Bonds are ahead of stocks in seniority. By law and contractually, bond interest must be paid before dividends. You're earning NOTHING if interest is > than EBITDA!

The bond market often does an intelligent job of compensating you for risk—you can actually SEE from the market rates of interest. A municipal bond with a current yield of 6% versus an original coupon of 4% means the market has sold off the bond to compensate more for the perceived risk. Simplistically speaking, that municipality pays $40 per year per 1000 face (4%), but now that $40 represents a 6% yield, the bond is trading at 666.6.

A BB-rated bond yields 6.09% (high yield) as of this writing, and BBB+ yields 5.4%. A stock should, intuitively, have a discount rate higher than this.

Earnings can GROW, and bond interest almost always is fixed. So, you are being compensated for the risk by being entitled to, but not guaranteed, all that is left over.

How to think about Stages of growth. For high-growth companies, the tendency has been to model and generate crazy numbers that imply companies are bigger than the addressable market. Look out for 5 years, arbitrarily, and think about how large the company can be and what the right/most realistic margin is. That's difficult. But just looking at a PE is telling you some multiple, the inverse of a yield, just like the bond yield.

Ultimately, it's a toaster. This great insight comes from Professor Bruce Greenwald, value investing legend at Columbia Business School (videos of his incredible lectures are available online). In the long run, because of competition and because of size, your business will be a GDP grower—it can't grow in excess of the economy forever, so it'll grow in line with (or maybe even more slowly than) the economy at large. Everything is commoditized or competed away (remember Schumpeter and Porter?)

When I first came into the market, the risk premium for stocks implied a 12-15% discount rate. In other words, I'd want at LEAST that kind of reward to take the risk of owning equities. Let's see what that means to a stream of earnings growing at 5% per year.

		1	2	3	4	5	Terminal Value	Perpetual Growth	2%
free cash flow	7%	100,000,000.00	107,000,000.00	114,490,000.00	122,504,300.00	131,079,601.00	1,310,796,010.00		
discount	10%	1.1	1.21	1.331	1.4641	1.61051	1.61051	(this = CF/(k-g)	
		90,909,090.91	88,429,752.07	86,018,031.56	83,672,085.24	81,390,119.28	813,901,192.79		
		1,244,320,271.84	Total cash flows						
		12.443	implied multiple						

Here's a company with a 10% discount rate assumed and 7

7% income growth in the first 5 years, collapsing to 2% growth. The implied multiple of free cash is 12.443x. You would pay no more than this. Increase the earnings assumption to 15% (doubling in that 5-year period), and you get a multiple of 15.8x. Keep that 15% growth rate and demand a 15 multiple, and you end up with a 10% multiple you'd pay for the company.

In a world where the spread of high yield over the long term is only 3%, one could argue that a discount rate of 15% or even 10% is too high for equities. Look what happens if you cut that to 7%

		1	2	3	4	5	Terminal Value	Perpetual Growth	2%
free cash flow	15%	100,000,000.00	115,000,000.00	132,250,000.00	152,087,500.00	174,900,625.00	2,498,580,357.14		
discount	7%	1.07	1.1449	1.225043	1.31079601	1.402551731	1.402551731	(this = CF/(k-g)	
		93,457,943.93	100,445,453.75	107,955,394.22	116,026,825.56	124,701,728.41	1,781,453,262.97		
		2,324,040,608.84	Total cash flows						
		23.240	implied multiple						

You end up with a 23 multiple.

That's the same 23-type multiple you're seeing in the market right now for many companies (like McDonald's). The market "thinks" 23 is right. SO, another use of the DCF is to test assumptions. Start with that 23 and see what it actually implies for earnings growth through the next 5 years and into the "terminal growth" phase in which the company collapses into GDP-like earnings growth.

The ultimate use of the DCF is triangulation and inversion.

Triangulation. With triangulation, your DCF will ultimately spit out a valuation. Check that against

P/E and P/S multiples both historic and cross sectionally across the industry.

Inversion. Assuming a constant discount rate and the CURRENT price, what kind of earnings is the stock discounting?

Inversion. The work of Michael Mauboussin and Aswath Damodaran (look them up on the internet and read/follow their work) is extremely important here because they cover the implied multiples and make great academic arguments around the use of DCFs.

We have the ingredients necessary now to value a business using discounted cash flow methods and triangulate them using other methods. I use them all. The beauty of the DCF is that it forces you to think about future periods and test how feasible (or how silly) your assumptions about the future are. Can a company really grow as quickly as management and the street say it could? Is a company really in the competitive situation a LOW multiple implies? Having a variant perception comes from doing the work and understanding where the market might have it wrong. A high multiple may be absolutely appropriate and NOT indicative of an expensive stock that should be shorted, just as a low multiple might be a signal of something awful. About to be stale bread comes at a 50% discount. So, too, to stocks that ultimately become 100 baggers.

We have the tools, but where do we find the financial information, both qualitative and quantitative, and where can we get it for free? Read on.

Oh, and if you want to bat around ideas with me, contact me at brian@broadwaycap.com. This is a collaborative business for me, NOT a competitive one.

CHAPTER 9
WHERE TO FIND FINANCIAL INFORMATION

I've given you the blueprint for determining a valuation for a company. To recap, you need to figure out what 1) free cash flow is, 2) how long you think it can grow at a super normal rate, and 3) what the appropriate discount rate is to use. The clue to 3 is art—you must look at prevailing bond yields, take a long-term view of the "price of time," and understand that in the denominator, you're making a judgment about the riskiness of the asset producing the denominator. THIS is the margin of safety.

If you can come up with a range of possible cash flow outcomes AND risk them appropriately, you have a working DCF.

Then you have a tool that can be compared to the easy-to-find PE, P/S and even EV/EBIT for your gut check.

Where can you find data related to cash flow, FOR FREE? The SEC mandates that companies produce these data.

Remember the guy who used to come on TV talking about his book "Free Stuff from the Government"??? He used to jump around in front of Capitol Hill talking about various grants and things you could get from "Uncle Sam—for FREE!!!" Well, the SEC.gov website is like that. You can build a billion-dollar fortune with its EDGAR system and a spreadsheet (heck, you can do it with a calculator and a pen, too).

Back at the turn of the millennium, almost a quarter century ago (!), obtaining financial information was about to be revolutionized. Yes, since the early 1930s, with the establishment of the SEC, public companies were required to publish some financial information, but until the dawn of the internet, that meant printing financials. I'm of the age where email addresses were first being issued to students (I graduated from Cooper Union in the class of 1998). A typical internet connection for an individual was still dial-up, and financials would come via fax machine. While EDGAR, the SEC's Electronic Data Gathering Analysis and Retrieval

When I was working as a broker in 1993-94, my mentor told me, "Call the company, ask for the recent annual report and the 10-Qs, give them our FedEx number so they can overnight them".

Now, you just need to go to sec.gov and the EDGAR system.

https://www.sec.gov/edgar/searchedgar/companysearch

Really, this website is all you need to have the "guts" of a model. If you feel that you are too easily manipulated by the qualitative, the quantitative elements are all there for you, and you can certainly build a quant-driven model off the information you can get here. There is a hell of a lot more information stored on the SEC's servers than on any chart screen.

Check this out on Starbucks

I'm writing this, incidentally, on Christmas day, with a Starbucks instant packet fueling the writing. It's fitting that the Federal Government is playing Santa with all this information. They force companies to stuff down the electronic chimney (sorry, I'm over-caffeinated). But, just LOOK what's here for your analyzing pleasure.

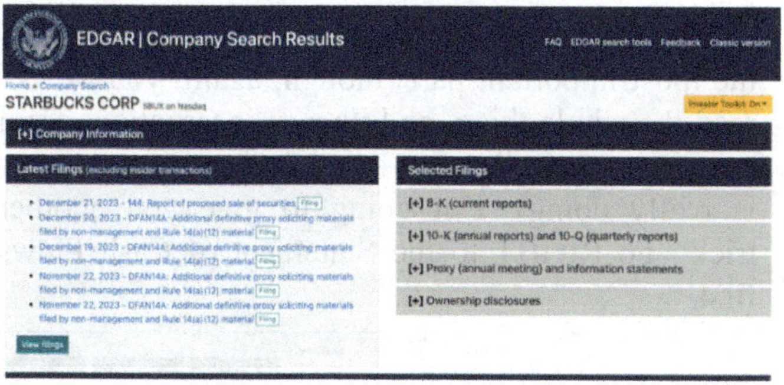

I like to start with the annual report, filed on Form 10-K

While I think DCF models are the "Queen of All Models" Form 10-K, the annual report is the "King of All Reports."

It's all laid out for you as if you are an owner or potential owner of the business. BECAUSE, YOU ARE!

Being focused heavily on the financials because I want to figure out what Starbucks is WORTH, I skip right to Item 8, the financial statements! Yes, I read the 10K cover-to-cover for every company I own and many, many more that I don't (such as the competitors-more on that later, where you can SEE how they are doing).

Since I've already admitted to you that I skip to the most important part (though, again, you MUST read the whole thing, and its past incarnations from prior years as well, to get a feel for how the company is really doing), I'm going to give you another trick—go RIGHT to the Statement of Cash Flows first.

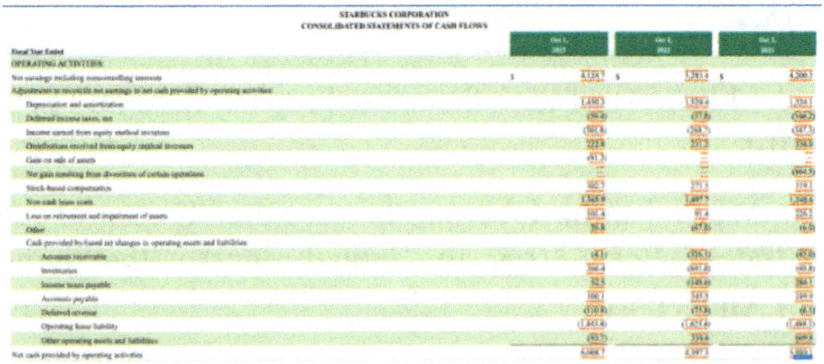
STARBUCKS CORPORATION
CONSOLIDATED STATEMENTS OF CASH FLOWS

Note here that Starbucks "threw off" $6 billion in operating cash flow in fiscal 2023 (which ended Oct 1, as you can see).

Capex's "additions to property plant and equipment" can be clearly seen in the cash from investing.

Without any adjustment—because you need to adjust to figure out what is "maintenance" capex and what is "growth" capex, the company simplistically generated $6 billion – 2.33 billion or 3.67 billion of free cash flow.

Starbucks currently has a market cap of $108 billion, so its free cash yield is just about 3%. But this is on unadjusted free cash flow.

What were the additions to PP&E? How much was allocated to growth and how much to maintain Starbucks "as is." I would bet that it is NOT the full 2.33 billion—THAT needs to be adjusted. If Starbucks is a zero-growth perpetuity (just growing in line with inflation), you can easily capitalize Starbucks at some discount rate and put the $3.67 billion in the numerator.

But what is growth for a chain of stores? Adding equipment within existing stores, like new coffee makers, cash registers, counters, etc. (we'll look at what kind of depreciable life these sorts of things have), but the real growth capex is new stores!

Starbucks is still growing, even from the large number of stores it currently operates (19,592 company-operated stores as of the end of the year, up from 18,253). Somewhere in that 2.33 billion of capex is the buildout cost of 1339 new Starbucks stores.

Company-operated store data for the fiscal year-ended October 1, 2023:

	Stores Open as of Oct 2, 2022	Opened	Closed	Transfers	Net	Stores Open as of Oct 1, 2023
North America:						
U.S.	9,265	483	(103)	—	380	9,645
Canada	946	43	(12)	—	31	977
Siren Retail	5	1	—	—	1	6
Total North America	10,216	527	(115)	—	412	10,628
International:						
China	6,019	857	(72)	—	785	6,804
Japan	1,630	110	(8)	1	103	1,733
U.K.	318	42	(5)	—	37	355
All Other	65	3	(1)	—	2	67
Siren Retail	5	—	—	—	—	5
Total International	8,037	1,012	(86)	1	927	8,964
Total company-operated	**18,253**	**1,539**	**(201)**	**1**	**1,339**	**19,592**

Writing this on Christmas morning, I asked one of my research analysts, Bob Cratchett (no, ChatGPT 4).

When reading a 10-K, I usually don't rely on an analyst's help, but it's irresistible to ask the question.

BR **You**

how much does it cost to open a new starbucks

ChatGPT

Based on a quick search, here's what I found.

Opening a Starbucks franchise involves a substantial investment and understanding of the company's unique business model. Starbucks doesn't operate traditional franchises; instead, they offer licensed store opportunities. The cost of opening a licensed Starbucks store can range significantly depending on various factors like location, size, and other expenses.

The initial investment for opening a licensed Starbucks store can vary from $228,620 to $2,888,700. This investment covers licensing fees, construction and build-out expenses, equipment and signage, initial inventory, and training expenses. Additionally, a licensing fee is typically required, averaging around $315,000. Moreover, potential licensees need to have a net worth of at least $700,000 to be considered.

This is a wide range (and, again, it's the cost for franchisees, not Corporate Starbucks. At the low end of this range ($226,000), these stores would cost a franchisee $228 million to build. I would assume that something like $500k per store is an appropriate sort of number.

Opening stores required GROWTH CAPEX! And I asked ChatGPT another question about the new store building for Starbucks and got the following:

> **ChatGPT**
> In 2023, Starbucks announced plans to open an average of eight new stores a day until 2030, as part of its long-term growth plan. This expansion aims to increase Starbucks' global presence to 55,000 locations by 2030, which includes adding approximately 17,000 new stores from the roughly 38,000 existing ones. This ambitious growth plan also involves a $3 billion efficiency program aimed at cutting costs, including $2 billion in cuts outside the store in costs-of-goods sold, and a $450 million investment in new technology for drink production efficiency. Starbucks' revenue for the last year was reported as $36 billion. The specific cost for new store openings in 2023 was not detailed in the available information.

https://www.cnbc.com/2023/11/02/starbucks-unveils-expansion-plans-cost-cutting.html#:~:text=Starbucks%20said%20Thursday%20it%20plans,by%20former%20CEO%20Howard%20Schultz.

The company is going to continue using this capex not only to grow but also to invest $3 billion over the next 7 years ($428 million a year) in cost-saving initiatives.

OK, we jumped OUT of the 10-K with the help of chatGPT to question specifics about the company's capex plan. We intuitively know that if the company continues investing at $2.3 billion for the next 10 years without opening new stores, there'd be $23 billion of unappreciated property plant and equipment out there.

Starbucks only HAS $7.3 billion of net PP&E on its balance sheet (I know this because I looked, as it's only a few pages before the cash flow statement). Over the past 3 years, the company has invested a total of $5.6 billion in PP&E (per the cash flow statement), but net PP&E has grown by substantially less, to $7.3 billion.

Depreciation is running such that the current PP&E would be depreciated down within 5 years! WE get that by dividing PP&E (7.3 billion) by depreciation (1.4 billion). There's at LEAST 900 million of growth capex in excess of depreciation, and I'm fairly convinced that Starbucks's current net PP&E won't entirely need replacing in 5 years.

Let's say for a minute that Depreciation and Amortization actually DO capture Starbucks's maintenance capex. Thus, free cash flow is actually $6 billion minus 1.4 billion or 4.6 billion. We are getting closer to what Starbucks looks like from a steady-state free cash flow basis, upon which to build the growth model.

Note that there is now something like $900 million—or more—of growth capex in the Starbucks plan, and we know the company is planning on opening 17k more stores on a base of 38k. That's a 44% increase in the number of stores. An overly-simple model would take into account what the average store does now and extrapolate. One could say revenues will increase 44% over the next 7 years, from 36 billion to nearly 52 billion. Right now, the 36 billion is producing 4.6 billion in free cash flow or 12.8% free cash margins. Keeping that margin flat would indicate $6.6 billion of free cash in 2030.

But, you say, first, there should be some operating leverage and second, the company mentioned a $3 billion cost savings initiative. Could we give it credit for that? Does Starbucks generate 9.6 billion in free cash in 2030, more than double the number now? That implies 44% revenue growth with 108% cash flow growth over the period.

Note that we want to get more rigorous in the analysis of store growth. We should understand that the next 17,000 stores are going to be different than the first 38,000. We should also note the composition of company-operated versus licensed (with the latter being typically much higher margin, lower revenue to the parent) as well as the operating leverage afforded by these.

We're talking a 7-year period. So, you raise the growth to (1/7) to get the annual growth. 5% topline growth over 7 years and 11.08% cash flow growth get us to those numbers. They don't sound terribly heroic, even off a base of $36 billion in sales.

Back to gut checks. Has Starbucks achieved this sort of thing before? Is 9.6 billion reasonable? 18.5% margins? According to FinBox, McDonald's operates at 31% free cash margins. Remember, though, that Starbucks has 82% company-owned stores, while only 5% of McDonald's are. Later, we'll talk about common size analysis to see if our gut is true.

Starbucks went public in 1992 with 165 stores. They ended this year with 38000. That's a 19.9% cagr! What about over the last 10 years? They grew from 19,767 to the current 38,000, a 6.8% cagr. So, this 5% store growth they target from that point would be a deceleration of that rate.

Item 8. Financial Statements and Supplementary Data

STARBUCKS CORPORATION
CONSOLIDATED STATEMENTS OF EARNINGS
(in millions, except per share data)

Fiscal Year Ended		Sep 29, 2013
Net revenues:		
Company-operated stores	$	11,793.2
Licensed stores		1,360.5
CPG, foodservice and other		1,738.5
Total net revenues		14,892.2

Revenues were $14,892 million, and we finished this past fiscal year at $35,975 million so the revenue cagr was actually 9.2%. Cash flow this year was over 6 billion, and in 2013, it was 2.9 billion, a 7.5% increase. Not the level of operating leverage I would have expected. However, 2013 had two large charges within the operating cash flow line that appeared (and were) non-recurring—1 a 2.8 billion litigation charge (positive, so an inflow) that was indeed cash, but not recurring earnings 2. A 1.0 billion cash outlay for deferred taxes. The 2.9 billion really looks more like 2.9-2.8+1.0 or 1.1 billion. Operating cash thus rose something like 18% over the past decade.

NB—I did a bit of data mining. 10 years is a somewhat arbitrary point, though we are in a "base 10" world, and thus I started from 2013 to demonstrate my point that over a long run—a 10-year period, a 6.8% CAGR of stores drove a 9.2% revenue CAGR and an 18% Cash Flow CAGR. I would encourage you (and I do it myself) to plug in EACH of the past 10 years, work back a few more and look for deviations off this average—then examine other parts of the 10-K and other sources so you can think about how to model out the future.

I START with the cash flow statement as my hub, with both the income statement (that "Drives" it, with net income being the top line of your operating cash flow) and the balance sheet (which is "driven" by it) as the two main branches. The income statement is what is reported in the media when the company reports quarterly (they also put out the balance sheet and cash flow statement in the earnings release, but media focus on EPS). The cash flow statement, to me, shows what REALLY happens and is more familiar a feel to private companies and—to my mind, more valuable for the construction of a valuation. In my mind, the balance sheet should be read with the liabilities especially emphasized because, as Charlie Munger said, they are REAL. As an equity holder, consider that when they liquidate the assets, you'll get a fraction of what they are worth to SATISFY the liabilities as close to 100% as possible. So, in my mind, it is much more prudent to think in terms of the real cash generation of the company than the accrual stuff you see in the income statement.

Yes—in a "Ready, Fire, Aim" world (another phrase I borrowed from my mentor, Rick), shorthand EPS and revenue growth "beat" or "miss" is what the short-term-minded focus on. But just like hearing the score of last night's ball game doesn't really match being there for each pitch, this stuff only tells a summary. It's even worse than that because it's not even an apples-to-apples score versus other companies AND is often distorted from period to period.

10Ks are not the only free source--10Qs

The next most important statement after the 10K is the quarterly (hence the Q, I suppose) 10Q. Three of these come out per year and have the same financial statements you'll find in the K, only for the quarter.

The Proxy Statement

https://www.sec.gov/Archives/edgar/data/829224/000082922423000007/a2023proxystatementfinal.htm

I like to read proxy statements because they give me, a shareholder, a sense of what the board looks like, how the company pays its management and how they feel they are doing against benchmarks (such as competitors). It even gives me a glimpse into who they think their competition is.

You can tell here how much skin in the game management has in terms of the number of shares and options they own. You can even see proposals from shareholders outside the board.

Here's how Starbucks compensates its new CEO

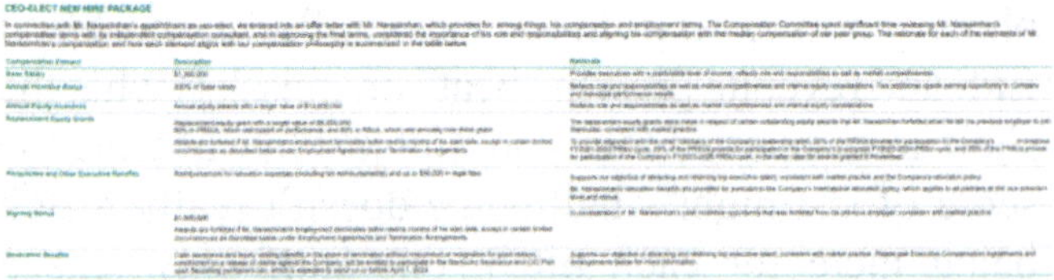

Starbucks spends 90 pages (!) in its proxy discussing the different drivers of how its top management is compensated and the different targets it aims to achieve.

But this isn't the only place where the company sets its goals. And you don't need to fly to the headquarters to get them.

Earnings presentations, where the management comes out quarterly to discuss results, are archived and often transcribed on the company's website (it's not mandated, though—note that Berkshire only does ONE annual meeting a year and no earnings calls, and they've done just fine). But

Annual report with pictures

The annual letter penned by Warren Buffett is the ultimate shareholder letter, and we've been gifted with them since the late 1970s.

https://www.berkshirehathaway.com/letters/letters.html

No one can come close, and I believe that there are extremely capable CEOs out there who do an incredible job without any of the literary genius that is Warren Buffett. I think we should all hope that other CEOs could write like him, and the world is a better place for having him as the benchmark, but after 25 years of doing this, I have not seen too many at THAT level.

However, just because they don't write as well as Warren Buffett doesn't mean that other companies don't have VERY useful annual letters AND very helpful annual reports that enhance the experience of the 10-K.

Some that are DEFINITELY worth reading include Amazon (Jeff Bezos), JPMorgan (Jamie Dimon), Starbucks (Howard Schultz, now retired), Microsoft (Satya Nadella) and Apple (Tim Cook).

Companies publish and often stream live to public conferences and roadshow presentations and have them up on the investor relations website.

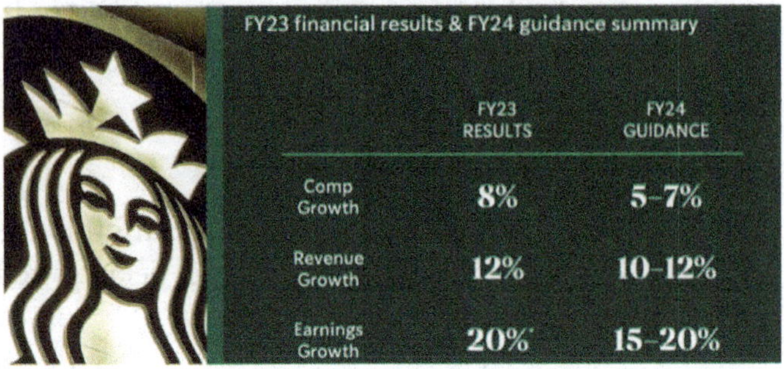

I'm all about subtraction, so when they are highlighting things, think about what they are NOT highlighting and what a competitor would like to hear.

https://stories.starbucks.com/uploads/2019/01/AboutUs-Company-Timeline-1.6.21-FINAL.pdf

CHAPTER 10
HOW TO READ MD&A AND OTHER 10-K NUGGETS.

Back in 1994, when I was first introduced to how to pitch a stock idea at Alex Brown & Sons, I was encouraged by my mentor there to read the annual reports AND to review his summaries of them, which he'd distilled into one-pagers.

Over the years, I've recognized the value of distilling an investment case to one page. Sure, these are complex companies with thousands of employees. But in the case of Exxon, they're basically extracting hydrocarbons, converting them into a useful form, transporting, marketing and ultimately selling them. In the case of McDonald's, they are seeking to convert raw materials such as beef, wheat, potatoes and corn (in syrup form) into calories that ultimately sell to consumers. Starbucks is there to addict you to high-quality coffee—itself a commodity.

Aside from the annual letter to shareholders, some of which I've mentioned in the prior chapter, the MD&A is an excellent source of information for the business.

Past Present Future

The MD&A gives the management a chance to highlight how the business NOW compares to the past and gives some idea of how the future can unfold.

Let’s look at McDonald’s MD&A.

It starts with a glossary—defined terms are laid out so the reader knows what they’re discussing.

MANAGEMENT'S VIEW OF THE BUSINESS

After nine chapters together, this won’t come as a surprise—I jumped ahead to the final defined term, and it's one that warms my heart: 'free cash flow'! Clearly, management wants to focus on it.

Free cash flow, defined as cash provided by operations less capital expenditures, and free cash flow conversion rate, defined as free cash flow divided by net income, are measures reviewed by management in order to evaluate the Company’s ability to convert net profits into cash resources, after reinvesting in the core business, that can be used to pursue opportunities to enhance shareholder value. Refer to the reconciliations in Exhibit 99.1 to this Form 10-K for further information on the Company's calculations of free cash flow and free cash flow conversion rate.

Later, we’ll go into the exhibits and footnotes, but let’s stick with the MD&A for MCD right now.

The second to last in the list is ROIC. This is like the toy in the Happy Meal box!

There is a reason I consider McDonald’s to be one of my favorite companies to analyze, and that is besides the fact that I've been eating Happy Meals since they were released in 1979, coinciding with kindergarten. Incidentally, one of my early Happy Meal memories is their tie-in with Star Trek The Motion Picture.

Remember, in our analysis of Starbucks in the last chapter, we discussed store growth and same-store sales.

2022 FINANCIAL PERFORMANCE

In 2022, global comparable sales increased 10.9%, primarily due to strong sales performance across all segments from continued execution of the *Accelerating the Arches* strategy

Note that the comparable sales (those stores 13 months in existence, grew sales 10.9%). A plethora of good questions should come from this, including "How much of this is due to pricing versus volume? What was the mix of products? Was last year a soft year relative to the prior year on each of the above). Oh, and not to skip too far ahead, but also to check out how their competitors (like Wendy's, Burger King, etc) did. Take notes, and remember, there is a 10-K for the prior year to review as well—and as far back as the company has been public.

Let’s scoot over to Starbucks and see how their MD&A talks about revenue growth.

Starbucks's results for fiscal 2023 demonstrate the overall strength of our brand. Consolidated revenues increased 12% to $36.0 billion in fiscal 2023 compared to $32.3 billion in fiscal 2022, primarily driven by strength in our U.S. business and growth in our International segment, partially offset by the impact of unfavorable foreign currency translation.

For both the North American segment and the U.S. market, comparable store sales increased 9% for fiscal year 2023 compared to an increase of 12% in fiscal year 2022. Average tickets for both the North America segment and the U.S. market grew 6%, primarily driven by pricing in our U.S. market

Here, Starbucks is breaking out not only comp store sales (AKA same-store sales) but also discussing average ticket increases. When modeling Starbucks’s growth, consider that they are adding different “parts” to the day, including lunches, and these can carry higher average selling prices. Currency is difficult to model but must obviously be considered in multinational companies. We’re trying to be roughly right, not precise, remember.

Pay special attention to the outlook in the annual report as well and see what management thinks the future holds.

Footnotes

Another fertile area for ideas about the company can be found within the footnotes. Again, I like to do the back-to-front type of reading with footnotes because there are so many.

Risk Factors/Competitors

Within the 10-K, a lot of risk factors can be characterized as "boilerplate," but not all of them.

The next step is to build a list and go to THEIR competitors' anuual reports.

The ultimate goal is to build a mental web of competitors and suppliers, and to the extent that they are public, even better because you can then read THEIR annual and quarterly reports to get your "gut check."

Action step

At this point, you are able to review an annual report (10-K), quarterly report (10-Q) and proxy statement and look for the right pieces in the management commentary, risk factors, and footnotes to understand key performance indicators and drivers for the business you're analyzing. Moreover, you're also able to look at "comps"—both competitors AND comparables, to the extent they are public and review their reports.

Pick a 10-K from a company you're considering analyzing, and with a pen, go to the MD&A, the risk factors, the footnotes and underline pieces that you find to be important.

CHAPTER 11
SCUTTLEBUTT

Phil Fisher, one of Buffett's (and my) great investing heroes, pioneered and named the "Scuttlebutt Method" of gathering information about investments. This was additive to the statistical approaches (valuation and margin of safety) launched by Benjamin Graham in Security Analysis.

Here are the essentials—the research analyst (you) should build or refute your case by talking to customers, vendors, management, competitors, and former employees and considering the entire industry. Build the mind maps we've discussed in the prior chapter, but this time including the

But how do you, the individual investor, a "mere mortal," talk to customers, vendors, management, competitors, and former employees?

SURE, The professional can have an advantage at his or her fingertips due to budget, reach, and name brand, but I believe this is not a major one. This is because I know—for a fact—that small firms with limited resources and NO brand are routinely able to TROUNCE the performance of the name brand firms that employ hundreds of millions for their research budgets.

And you can, too.

Idea Generation and picking up data on your own ideas, being a Scuttlebutt King or Queen starts with YOU.

First, there is a physical element. You will need to get off your butt and do some work. But you are already doing the work every minute of the day.

You wake up and look at your watch. Mine's an Apple watch. I eschewed brands like Rolex not because they are not incredible machines but because I often walk into doorways and have smashed fancy watches. Jot down what watch you're wearing because whoever sold you that watch is a good source of information. The kid at the Apple Store (a literal and figurative Genius) helped me set it up. Actually, it runs on a network, which is brought to me by AT&T (T). The young man in the AT&T store actually helped me move away from Verizon (VZ) after twenty years. Even if you don't have an Apple watch, I guarantee you're being served by a cellular carrier, and most of the major ones are public. Within both my watch and my smartphone are components that are produced by many different public companies, and the

Flip the light switch. The power likely reached your house through copper wire. There are multiple public companies that mine for that (such as Freeport-McMoRan and Southern Copper), and the utility that provides your power is also public. You might have bought that lamp at Amazon (AMZN) or the fixtures at Lowes or Home Depot.

Go to the shower. No—I don't think you need one, my sweet-smelling reader, but I believe you'll find products made by Procter and Gamble, Unilever, L'Oreal, Colgate Palmolive, and even Berkshire Hathaway (Gilette).

You stayed up late reading this book, so you have a hangover with all the excellent ideas I gave you (BUD can do this too). Bayer makes the aspirin you might take. After shaving with your Gillette razor, you cut yourself, so a Johnson & Johnson bandage comes to the rescue. Keep that toilet and tub clean with Clorox products. You walked out of the bathroom, and I'm guessing you bought a lot of those products at Target (TGT), Walmart (WMT) or Amazon (AMZN). You can buy all of the above at any of the above.

Before I hit the shower, I usually have a coffee, sometimes a few. I enjoy private brands (I live part of the year in Panama), but when I don't, I am partial to Starbucks (SBUX) (there it is again). My wife gets her caffeine from Coca-Cola (KO). My son prefers his water when he's home from college, but that is also a KO product.

When my mother-in-law visits, she uses the Keurig (also public) machine I bought specifically for her.

You haven't even put your work clothes on, and you've encountered how many public companies?

Here's your assignment. Before you get in your car (which is probably made by a public company with a bunch of parts made by other public companies), I want you to list every product you consume AND where you bought it. It is important to put on the mindset of understanding WHY you chose the products you did versus their competition, who makes the competition (why does Monica drink Coke Zero versus Pepsi's equivalent? Why do I drink

Starbucks versus Dunkin?) Actually, I drink BOTH Starbucks AND Dunkin, depending on the day.

Whenever you make the buying decision, part of your new mindset as Scuttlebutt Royalty is to take notes as to why you are and try to ask questions of the person selling you the stuff (or, when you're buying online, check reviews of that and the competing products).

Get dressed and consider what companies produced your clothes and your shoes. Where did you buy them? For women, there's a strong possibility your purse is made by one of the LVMH (public) brands.

Your transportation

Stand in front of your car and question how you picked the BMW (public, in Germany, under BMW) over the Lexus (Toyota) versus the neighbor who bought the Tesla (TSLA). Your car dealer, next time you are in, and your mechanic will tell you all about why one car is better/worse than the other. Go back to Chapter 10, and you'll figure out how to find what suppliers are in that car.

On your ride, you may pass fast food vendors and stores like Walmart and Target. Check out who has the biggest lines. Drive carefully. Or maybe take a UBER or LYFT (both public). I walk when I'm home in New York, so I get to see firsthand what stores are doing.

Malls

Skip work today and go to the mall or the shopping districts of your city (like Fifth Avenue and

Soho in my hometown). I find the mall to be one of my favorite places to gauge consumer behavior. Before the rise of shopping on the internet 25 years ago, this was really the ONLY place to gauge consumer behavior. You can not only see what brands people are wearing, you can go to stores and see what they are BUYING and even pester (ok, be nice) clerks and managers with questions. My wife can walk by stores that are empty and open, with a high batting average, about which ones are shorts.

Big Stores

Supermarkets and "big box retailers" such as Costco, Walmart, and Home Depot are my other favorite spots to hang out and figure out consumer trends/do my scuttlebutt. Before you even walk in, you can observe, again, what people are driving and wearing and watch them exit with what they're buying. Catch trends about what they're eating. Talk to the people working in the Home Depot or Lowes about what kind of projects are being bought for.

Your vacation

Your next trip out of town for a holiday is a great chance to observe trends around the world and around the country. You should have a notebook with you because you'll be able to jot down what you're seeing, even at the airport.

On domestic trips, I'm able to do the same walking around Scuttlebutt that I do at home, visiting chain stores, restaurants, malls, and supermarkets to see what people are doing in different regions. I take note of how full the airport is (FAA.gov gives you the ability to do this at home) and how full the plane is. I try to check out what kind of sneakers the kids are wearing, the purse brands, if I can identify them, and the brand of jackets. Americans love to have labels on stuff, so I'm able to identify a lot of different things. The food courts of airports typically have familiar and not-so-familiar brands, so I make a note of that. When I'm in different regions of the country, I am sure to check out the fast-food brands that aren't as familiar in New York, as well as the beverages (both alcoholic and non) that are being sold in stores.

International travel gives me a chance to do all of the above AND often catch trends before they come to the States. For instance, Monica discovered Zara in Spain before it came to the US. I was able to do a LOT of due diligence on OXXO (part of Femsa, FMX) as well as multiple foreign carriers and auto companies (such as Renault) by visiting Mexico and France. Before Alfa Romeo (part of Stellantis, then Fiat) was re-introduced to the US, I rented one in Italy and drove it to Croatia. My then-four-year-old son didn't like the handling.

None of this is a statistically significant poll. You can't actually draw a conclusion about this quarter's car sales (if that's what you like to forecast, but I am fairly certain it's not a great use of your time and not really the basis of good investing practices anyway) based on a four-year-old New York kid leveling verdict on Alfa Romeo's stiffness across Slovenian foothills. But, seeing what brands are emerging, what ones are hot, what brands are not hot, what brands are getting destroyed, and understanding the crucial question of how a brand can get unseated are all open to you if you do the exploring.

The Internet—Scuttlebutter's dream.

Before the internet enabled ANYONE to do investment research from their couch, without spending anything but your time (and some electricity and whatever your ISP charges you), you actually DID need to go out, go on trips, walk around malls and supermarkets to understand the choice.

Every single public company I mentioned earlier in the chapter has more than one internet presence for marketing. Let's consider Anheuser Busch InBev . Of course, there is the investor relations website, just like every other public company. However, there are also national and brand sites.

Brand	Country of Origin	Official Website
Budweiser	United States	www.budweiser.com
Stella Artois	Belgium	www.stellaartois.com
Corona	Mexico	www.corona.com
Beck's	Germany	becks.de
Leffe	Belgium	leffe.com
Hoegaarden	Belgium	handfamilycompanies.com/hoegaarden
Modelo	Mexico	www.modelousa.com
Michelob	United States	www.michelobultra.com
Bud Light	United States	www.budlight.com
Skol	Brazil	www.skol.com.br

This table provides a quick reference to the official websites of the top 10 Anheuser-Busch InBev brands, along with their countries of origin.

I used ChatGPT4 to help. Here's what I did.

ChatGPT

To find the official websites for the top 10 Anheuser-Busch InBev brands, I followed these steps:

1. **Search Queries**: I conducted individual searches for each brand, using the format " [Brand Name] beer official website". This specific phrasing helped target the official pages.
2. **Selection of Sources**: From the search results, I selected relevant links. I primarily chose links that directly referred to the brand's official page or those from reputable sources pointing to the official website.
3. **Verification**: I clicked on the chosen links to verify that they led to the official websites of the respective brands.
4. **Compiling Information**: I then compiled the URLs into a list, aligning them with the brand names and countries of origin.
5. **Final Check**: I ensured the URLs matched the correct brands and were functional.

This process was repeated for each brand to create a comprehensive list of their official websites.

You can do this for Bud's competitors as well. This replaces the job of a junior analyst or intern.

Since I like investing in automotive companies and the supply chain, I did this for Stellantis.

You

Do not do a quick search. Make a table of the top 10 Stellantis Brands in one column, that brand country of origin in second column and URL in third column. You can get some of that information here: https://www.stellantis.com/en/brands/our-brands. use whatever search methods you employ but I need a table with 3 columns--please give your answer in that exact form. Thanks!

ChatGPT

Based on the information from the Stellantis website, here's a table of their top 10 brands, the country of origin for each, and the URL for the brand's official website:

Brand	Country of Origin	Official Website
Abarth	Italy	www.abarth.com
Alfa Romeo	Italy	www.alfaromeo.com
Chrysler	United States	www.chrysler.com
Citroën	France	www.citroen.com
Dodge	United States	www.dodge.com
DS Automobiles	France	www.dsautomobiles.co.uk
Fiat	Italy	www.fiat.com
Jeep	United States	www.jeep.com
Lancia	Italy	www.lancia.com
Maserati	Italy	www.maserati.com

Among other things, I am a Certified Prompt Engineer and created this prompt for analyzing the company at a high level. This information is also usually available in the 10-K.

Brand	Country of Origin	Official Website
Coca-Cola	United States	us.coca-cola.com
Diet Coke	United States	www.dietcoke.com
Fanta	Germany	www.fanta.com
Sprite	United States	www.sprite.com
Costa Coffee	United Kingdom	www.costa.co.uk
Dasani	United States	www.dasani.com
Powerade	United States	www.powerade.com
Minute Maid	United States	www.minutemaid.com
Simply	United States	www.drinksimplybeverages.com
Topo Chico	Mexico	www.topochicousa.net

For my scuttlebutt purposes, I am in the process of creating apps for ChatGPT to enable this quick and dirty analysis of brands within a business.

Consider Social Media

Plus, there's the company's social media presence: Instagram, Facebook, and even Twitter(X).

Also, for this company, you can go to LinkedIn and find the company's HR site, as well as executives, people who work there, and people who work with and at competitors. I can write an entire book (and will aim to, someday soon) to teach you all I know about using THIS resource for networking.

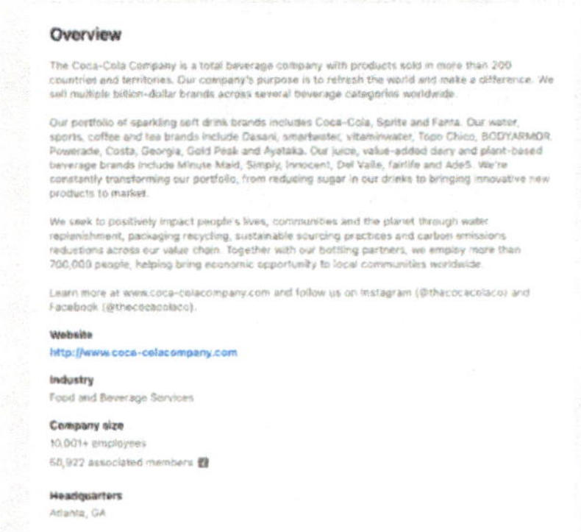

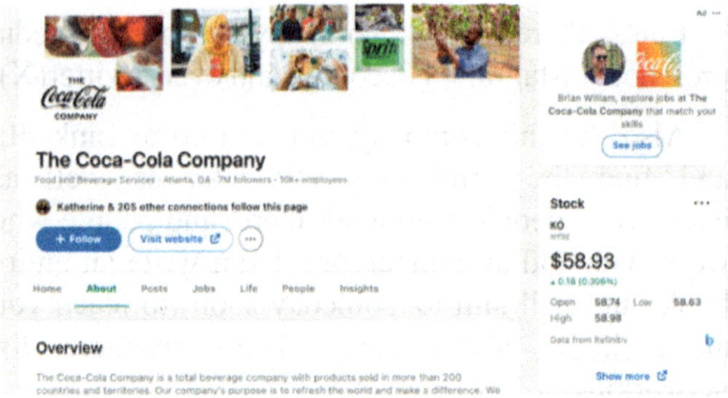

NOTE: 206 connections of mine follow KO.

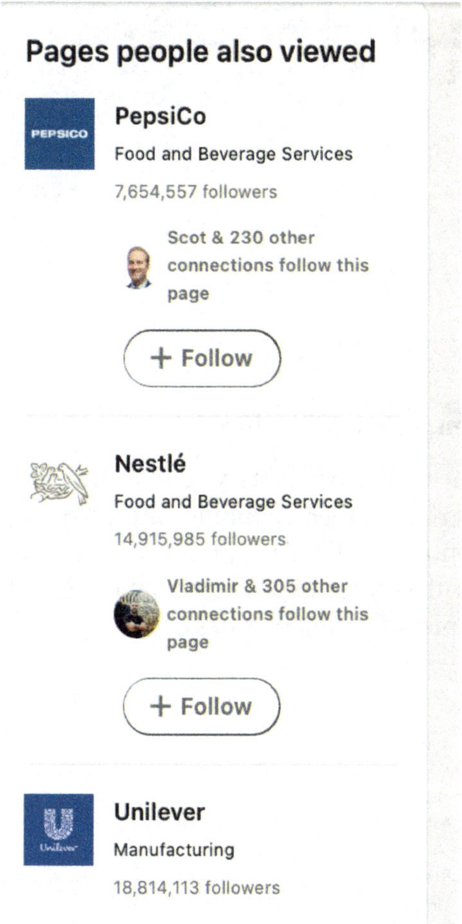

LinkedIn suggests other sites to follow as well. And I, like you, have a lot of friends, and they follow these "comps."

All of this can be done FOR FREE.

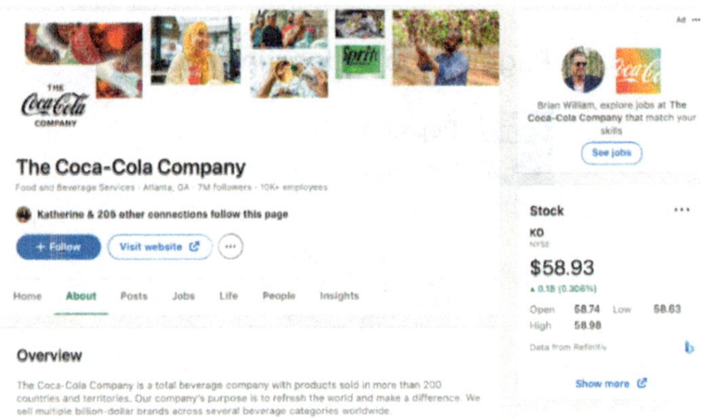

Amazon, other sales sites

A lot of the products you consume are sold via Amazon and other shopping sites. You can search Amazon in real time for prices on branded products (easy with consumer products, not relevant for things like semiconductors or ships).

Based on the number of visits, the top e-commerce websites in the US as of 2024 are:

1. **Amazon** - With approximately 5.2 billion monthly visits, Amazon is the most visited e-commerce site.
2. **eBay** - Following Amazon, eBay boasts around 1.7 billion visits per month.
3. **Alibaba Group** - A leading Chinese e-commerce website with a significant number of visits.
4. **Rakuten** - Based in the UK, it's known for deals with coupons and rebates.
5. **Walmart** - A well-known retail giant, receiving 466.2 million visits in January 2022.
6. **Etsy** - A global marketplace for unique and creative products.
7. **PinDuoDuo** - A large agriculture-focused technology platform in China.
8. **Costco** - Known for its diverse wholesale products.
9. **Target** - One of the oldest and largest discount retailers in the US.
10. **Best Buy** - Specializes in consumer electronics.
11. **Shopify** - A popular e-commerce platform based in Ottawa.
12. **Flipkart** - One of India's biggest e-commerce platforms.
13. **Allegro** - A major online shopping brand in Poland.
14. **Taobao** - A large C2C marketplace in China.
15. **Avito.ru** - A Moscow-based classifieds company.

If you're studying travel, sites like Expedia, Hopper, and Booking.

Old Media is still relevant and helpful.

Because I live in multiple countries, I had to move my print subscriptions to the WSJ, Barrons, FT, Economist and pretty much every other print thing to digital. You may still get your physical local or national newspaper. These are amazing sources of advertising and marketing information that you should use for your file. Check the weekend circulars, the ad copy and how your companies and competitors are positioning themselves.

Also, you're likely still receiving TONS of physical mail per year, even though we are squarely in the world of e-commerce.

Mail catalogs, like Sears still come into your mailbox. Pay attention to them, and also pay attention to direct marketing that comes in the mail, TV, Even terrestrial radio. All these media give you a chance to see how the companies are marketing.

Competitors

As we covered in the prior chapter, the 10-K often lists the company's biggest competitors. Of course, it's easy to look at Ford versus GM, Toyota and Honda, McDonald's versus Burger King and Wendy's and Walmart versus Target.

Your own business

If you are working for a public company, check with your compliance department about trading in your company's shares. I am not an attorney nor a compliance professional, and you should speak with them and also thoroughly review your own company's policies before doing anything related to trading in your employer's stock. If you work for a private company with access to privileged and proprietary information about a public company, this sort of conversation is also important to have. Examples of firms that DO have this sort of information include professional service firms (law, consulting, accounting) as well as suppliers. There are so many public companies out there, actually, tens of thousands of them, that you don't want to risk being in trouble trading on insider information. And you don't need to!

Use your own business sense and connections to build a proprietary list of information anyone with hard work can produce without running afoul of the rules. Checking parking lots or asking salespeople at electronics stores or waiters at casual dining restaurants how things are doing is NOT going to get you in trouble. Common sense is often the best way to be on the right side of things.

Others

As you're doing your research, you should involve your family, your friends, your neighbors, and members of your clubs. My friends know me as an investment nerd, but you don't have to become a nerd to sleuth around and become a great investment conversationalist. And it's quid pro quo—you can tell them what you're working on (BE VERY CAREFUL ABOUT PITCHING IDEAS TO FRIENDS TOO HEAVILY, BECAUSE THEY

ONLY REMEMBER THE LOSERS). Conversation starters include asking about their car, their shoes, their cellphone, what video games their kids like, etc.

Trips to stores as a family and even shopping on the internet together (or asking family and friends what they're doing) are ways to find new ideas and research existing ones.

There is a mindset here that of being a detective, someone curious like a scientist, testing your theories about the company's competitive position, marketing strengths and weaknesses, building what has been called "the mosaic" of information throughout the scuttlebutt process. Like everything in investing, it's iterative—you never just build a model once. You keep refining it to reflect updated reality and probabilistic scenarios as well as key performance indicators, new sources of competition, etc.

As we opened the book, you need to be contrarian, to be independent. How do you maintain this mindset? In the next chapter, I'll discuss some ideas on how to keep this momentum and discipline. This is beyond a hobby. This is a mission.

Notice that thus far, nothing has been outside the reach of a normal education, and all of it is free. You will NEVER reach perfection at financial statement analysis, screening, valuation, and due diligence, but neither—really-will anyone else. These are all iterative and constant learning situations.

CHAPTER 12
MINDSET

"Baseball is 90 percent mental. The other half is physical." Yogi Berra

Investing is quite like baseball in this respect. The physical part is probably not half—in fact, Charlie Munger's concept of "sit on your ass investing" is appealing to those seeking convexity. I opened the book with a challenge to you: are you a contrarian? We have established that you are.

Contrarianism is a mental state and a choice. You do not follow the consensus. That can be frightening. It can also be VERY annoying. Why is that? We all crave popularity on some level. We all crave belonging on some level. I look at my dog, Donny. He's a pack animal. You cannot take the wolf out of him—he's there to protect and lead his "pack," and I see it in how he protects my mother-in-law, my wife and plays rough with his "brother," my human son. He leads ME even though I'm part of the pack that delivers food and treats. We are social as well, and the worst thing about being hardwired for society is that picking stocks that are consensus, while definitionally setting us up for average returns, is what most of us are wired to do.

But you know better. And I do, too.

It doesn't make owning a stock that underperforms crypto or the hottest profitless "unicorn" stock that comes up at Thanksgiving dinner. In your mind, with both, you need to ask these questions—does this person really KNOW how they made money? Can they repeat that, and—if they are so smart and not rich, why not?

Envy plays a role. A corollary to belonging is the need deep within all of us to envy someone else's real or apparent success.

So, can you eliminate both the need to belong and the proclivity to envy? Can your significant other (or can you at least shut your significant other's voice out of your head when he or she starts raving about his or her cousin's latest coin victory).

It sucks to hold something that is underperforming, but that is EXACTLY what seeking convexity and asymmetry often condemns us to do. I don't chase fads. I buy companies, preferably at a margin of safety. That margin of safety, as we saw, translates into lower multiples and/or prices that are lower than before (broken stocks, 52-week low lists, etc).

At the end of 2021, I was at a fantastic party for a retiring friend and was pitched NFTs (non-fungible tokens) as an "investment." Apparently, because Justin Bieber had paid up for a GIF of a monkey in sunglasses, this was the appropriate place to allocate client capital instead of the large position I initiated inputs on technology unicorns. I'd lived through 1999-2000 when I was NOT mature and suffered with art history majors making "life-changing" returns in dot com stocks day trading. It's easy to laugh about the NFT guys and the dot com guys now because the humiliation ultimately was theirs.

Meanwhile, value investing continues to pay AND offer opportunities.

But what is your mindset tells you why this must be? Isn't it safer to follow the crowd? If you still think so, you won't be stupid to buy an index fund. You STILL need to ignore the NFT and dot com type stuff—there WILL be speculative elements of owning an S&P500 index fund because these are 500 US companies all innovating in some way or another, but that'll be muted by the more mundane.

Why do I rule out things like NFTs, cryptos, 1999 tech stocks and the like? Because I cannot value the first two (tell me what monkey gif or cryptocurrency is worth), and I KNOW very well how to value the last one—and I got a chance to own a bunch of them in 2001-2003 as well as in the tech rout of 2022. The market—in my view—and that of many others I admire, has a mental condition of its own. The stages of market psychology follow a cycle—Optimism, Euphoria, Arrogance, Denial, Fear, Panic, and Caution. Consider that you also feel that way across a cycle. As Buffett has said, we have to be the market's master. And in order to do that, we need to master OURSELVES.

One way is to take what I've tried to dig out of you in the past 11 chapters—you have a toolkit, both quantitative and qualitative, that you'll be using to give yourself confidence in the actual VALUE of what you own. How much cash can a business or a product or segment within that business throw off under certain conditions, certain realms of probability? We have built mental maps around the moats of a business so we can feel confident in our assessment of how assailable those moats are. We have built working models outlining the outcomes under certain assumptions about revenue growth, cost movements, and capital expenditures. We have thought heuristically (rule of thumb) about different probabilistic scenarios.

So we are not flying blindly without a map—we've built the map.

Compare this to the guy who bought the Justin Bieber monkey. What competitive advantage did he assess? Did he really model cash flow scenarios with each scenario carefully considered? You now know how to do that. There's NO WAY he can do that. Such 'investments' essentially rely on the 'greater fool' theory—the only profit you can derive from items like the monkey picture comes from another person paying more than what you initially paid. OK, so it's art, and thus it behaves like art, one could say. Not so fast—I can whip up a monkey gif as easily as that guy's. The supply of monkey gifs might be unlimited. These are not Van Gogh paintings. Oh, yes, I understand the use case of the blockchain and cryptography generally, and this stuff is a derivative of that. But, again, this is a tenuous relationship at best. And this is why the monkey things were lost.

But even if they WON, I still couldn't assess the value of the thing. That's my impediment. I'm happy having it. It's like having green eyes (which I do). I'd be a fool to spend my life regretting I don't have brown ones. I don't want to be a fool envying a guy who figured out how to flip a monkey coin to a guy willing to pay more for it.

That brings me to the concept of FOMO, fear of missing out, which drives a lot of the euphoria in the markets, is well researched and documented and—wonderfully—continues year after year to create bubbles that can be shorted. Companies are NOT monkeys because there is a limited supply of them and an often-large supply of speculators who can bid their shares up. Often, there is a high short interest, which—when combined with touts and some good "stories" (and often an accommodative monetary policy) can make these sorts of speculative companies' shares explode.

Earlier in my career, I'd attempt to short-sell these things (I am a contrarian), and I'd often get taken to the woodshed. Ultimately, bubbles do burst, but the pain of being squeezed is another emotion we need to think about. You can argue all you want about something being overvalued, but you need to get the timing right. In the next chapter, we'll talk about some rules of thumb for doing that.

Meanwhile, You need to consider some fictional heroes when you have your mindset. Visualization techniques based on movies are helpful.

First, there's Mister Spock. You need to cultivate a cool, detached, yet inquisitive nature. Notice Spock had a catchphrase "fascinating". You should approach wins and losses with that level of mental clarity.

Second, and staying within the space realm, is Han Solo. Smuggler. Somewhat impulsive but heroic in the end. Used his gut feeling and ability to ignore the odds (remember he had C3PO shut down when he was quoting odds against navigating the asteroid field). You need some degree of Han Solo in you—he was opportunistic, modifying his tools (the millennium falcon) to make him money, outrunning the imperial authorities. The ability to navigate through an asteroid field and ultimately contribute to the destruction of TWO Death Stars with limited resources is what makes this character worth emulating. You're a rebel when up against the death star that is the market (and a bunch of unnamed brokerage firms and underperforming funds).

Harrison Ford also gives us Indiana Jones. Investing is like his vocation—archaeology - in many respects. So much of our daily work reminds me of his search for the idol in the opening scenes of Raiders of the Lost Ark. There's certainly the element of Dr Jones in his university class as well. Our chosen field enables us to be both the professorial Dr Jones and the adventuring Indy, poison darts being fired at us as well. You NEED to be able to run into jungles to get these sorts of things (you don't need to fight a sword-wielding guy or snakes in Egypt, but it feels that way).

So, when you wake up in the morning, you want to be a blend of these guys—Spock, Han Solo and Indiana Jones.

Irwin M. Fletcher, the hero of the movie Fletch, is also someone whom I admire for his investigative skills. Adopting pseudonyms such as John Cocktoasten and Gordon Liddy, even telling a police chief that his occupation is "shepherd" is the way this investigative journalist foiled the bad guys and got the bad guy's girl (and his first-class tickets to Rio in the end).

This is all pretend. Make believe. But isn't that what we're trying to do, visualizing successful investments by working backward from scenarios we construct?

You are also an applied probabilist here. You're assessing the probabilities of different outcomes—NOT forecasting, but creating a series of "IF-THEN" statements and using what you know about the company's position to construct a valuation of that business.

In a very real sense, this is like horse handicapping. It's fitting that Buffett himself, as a kid, wrote handicapping sheets at the local Omaha horse track. Here, instead of looking at the condition of horses, the skill of jockeys, the past performance of both and the competitive field, you're substituting companies for horses, managements for jockeys and the competitive field of horses for real competitors. Things like muddy tracks at prior races have their analogs as well. But it's ultimately the same game. You're coming up with a price—a value of the company, using scenario analysis similar to that of calculating whether the odds of a horse are cheap enough to buy.

I continue to harp on the relationship between investing and building probability trees because most people don't seem full to embrace these ideas, relying instead on momentum and less on "Thinking in Bets," which is a fantastic book written by a real gambler, Annie Duke. Listen to the audiobook. You also must read the collected works of Nassim Taleb on the subject because the entire thing IS probability. The biography of Ed Thorp also gives insight, as does his hard-to-find "Beat the Market." The market truly has elements of blackjack and poker as well as horse racing, but it is NOT gambling the way some people portray it if you leave out "speculation" and focus on establishing a margin of safety using both the quantitative and quantitative tools we've worked through together. I find it helpful to consider investments as a series of bets with or without convex payouts. If they don't pass a test of convex payout, I move on. I'll talk more about that in the next chapter.

Back in 2020, launching a fund was either foolhardy or brilliant, but nevertheless, it was a lonely endeavor, like long-distance running (I imagine) or LeMans racing at night (I think about doing this a lot).

I did a lot of research since 2020 on improving my mindset. You can't pray or meditate your way into good performance, but if you come at your investing and trading angry or euphoric, you're going to make mistakes. Ray Dalio cites Transcendental Meditation as a main factor, explaining how he has been able to build one of the greatest track records of all time.

I was lucky to read the work of Jared Tendler, The Mental Game of Trading, www.jaredtendler.com, and it has worked wonders for the way I plan my day. One crucial thing he enabled me to do—and you'll be able to do it too—is to document your mental state and how you react and respond to your trading throughout the day through journaling.

Now, this is a book about investing, not trading for a living on a day-to-day basis—I am fully aware of that, and as both portfolio manager and trader for my fund, I wear both hats. However, even though YOU won't necessarily be trading 6.5 hours a day daily, the mental tactics and strategies Jared Tendler provides will prove INCREDIBLY useful. If you understand how you feel when you're doing your research and when you're doing the building of a position, you'll inevitably be able to understand if there were mental mishaps and how to correct them. You can control how you feel and how you react, but if you don't document them and take action steps (he gives you TONS of ways to address this), you will be somewhat rudderless. Tendler gives you a rudder.

In working through the Tendler book, I was introduced to the work of Brett Steenbarger, whom I also recommend reading.

In working on journaling and listening to great podcasts, I got turned on to Journalytic https://journalytic.com, which enables me to write down why I'm buying something and track the different thoughts and elements that go into making the buy decision.

The catharsis of writing a memo about why you want to own something is very important, if not crucial, to the practice of investing. I have handwritten tens of thousands of pages of notebooks as well as laptops full of memos about "what it is, what it's worth, how can I be wrong, what are the catalysts."

The most important thing to understand is that no matter how much you work on your positions, you will lose. There is risk in every single company you purchase. To paraphrase Charlie Munger--If you cannot mentally handle the near certainty that you can suffer a 50% drawdown, stay away. With that said, he did, and so did Berkshire, and they did fine.

Take a break. Walk around the block. And remember that there are no called strikes. And…

CHAPTER 13
IMPLEMENT!

You're now a warrior with the tools at your disposal, including how to screen for stocks, how to value businesses, how to look around financial statements, how to do research, and how to have the right mindset. As Nike's great ad campaign and slogan say, "Just do It."

It's fitting we should lead a chapter with this tagline because I just (December 2023) finished listening to the audible version of Shoe Dog, which was previously recommended at a Berkshire Annual Meeting and absolutely one of the best business books I read last year. How did a group of self-described Running Nerds build one of THE great brands and businesses of the past 50 years? Read the book, but certainly, they followed their own advice and did it. A singular focus on becoming the best sports shoe company in the world is one main theme of the book.

Sir Richard Branson has an expression, "screw it, let's do it," which comes from his incredible ability to jump into new lines of business (he's founded hundreds). His ability to move on from failure and to fund successes has contributed to his becoming a billionaire.

Neither billionaire Phil Knight nor Sir Richard were thumbsuckers. Unless you're born a billionaire, you cannot really be (and even then, to STAY a billionaire, you need to be a person of action).

One a Stanford MBA, trained accountant and accomplished athlete with a single company and one a high school dropout serial (and parallel) entrepreneur, they both had a HUGE bias for action.

And now you do because you're about to build a portfolio!

You have, as Taleb has put it, Skin in the Game. You're about to join the realm of people who don't BS because you have prepared, and you're about to buy positions in things you've researched and decided meet your margin of safety.

Easy, Right?

But how many of these, and what size should they be? How many longs and shorts and cash should I have? Is there a science to this? What if I only have 10 ideas?

First, you want to set a portfolio up in a barbell way. Have part in cash, part in conservative investments and part in more aggressive ones. The shape of the portfolio could have a certain percentage allocated to the most convex situations (things with very high reward: risk ratios).

You should be thinking of ALL of your positions in this regard. What is the valuation versus what is the price you're paying? Is the ratio 2:1, 3:1? More? Remember, you're aiming to buy 50 cent dollars, as a rule of thumb.

But can you enhance that return? One way is through options. Kids- do not try this at home. With call options, you end up with the ability to have exposure to almost all of the upside of a share for the entire time until the the option expires. Obviously, time is finite when you do this, so you have the added element of time decay.

Let's say you have calculated the value of Southwest Airlines to be $60. The stock is currently trading at $28.88. A fifty-cent dollar in your valuation work. Options exist all the way out to January 2026!

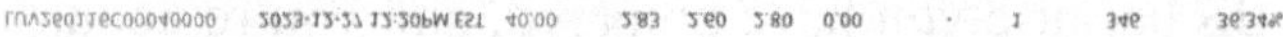

You have the ability, for $280, to buy the equivalent of 100 shares of Southwest and basically control $4000 worth of stock for the next 2 years. If you're right, if LUV is truly valued at 60, that $280 would trade for an intrinsic value of $2000.

I did similar with Exxon Mobil, which I valued at $120 back in 2021 when it was trading under $60. I was able to buy $75 strike calls that ultimately were trading for $25 apiece—a ten-bagger.

These are simplistic explanations and do not take into account the elements of options a more advanced study would take into account, such as volatility and other elements of extrinsic value. Since there is time between now and expiry, options with NO intrinsic value (like these LUV calls) trade as a function of the time and the volatility of the underlying security. Are these options "cheap" relative to what you think the stock is worth? Yes, if you think the stock is worth $60. These options allow you to buy at 42.60 and give you a chance to make 17.40 for each 2.60 you put up—a 6.8 bagger. Are they "cheap" relative to what an options pricing model will tell you? That's for the more advanced study you'd get from books and sites I recommend. For EXCELLENT primers on options pricing theory, go to tastylive.com, as well as read Taleb.

Options enable you to enjoy convexity while keeping cash handy. You can replicate an entire portfolio of longs using options, and there are a variety of combinations one can use to express their position on a stock; I love options.

In fact, I would love you to schedule a call -- contact me at brian@broadwaycp.com, and we can strategize about options together.

There's something called the put/call parity, which is a basis of my career and fund. A call is actually the equivalent of long stock plus LONG a put (you've protected your downside). Southwest could go to ZERO. If you put on this long-dated LUV position, you'd risk $260 per 100 shares. Not the 2800 you would risk if the stock were to fall to zero (and airlines CAN go bankrupt, though LUV has avoided this).

Incidentally, you can use options to hedge the portfolio as well and/or create paired trades. Suppose you think Coke is undervalued, but Pepsi is not, and further, you have determined that factors outside Coke's control could hurt both of them. You can express this long Coke calls and long Pepsi puts. Or, you think that Coke is undervalued, but the general market is overvalued—you can express this via long Coke calls and long ETF puts (SPX, QQQ, OIH etc.).

A $1 million portfolio could be replicated using perhaps 20% of capital using these methods, leaving

80% cash and some available to "hedge" out risks or to put shorts on the other side of the "barbell."

Sizing

Sizing positions is a function of your conviction. Again, you've determined your best names by ranking them as a percent upside/downside (or the reverse in the case of shorts).

I have looked at positions in terms of 3,5,7% positions on the long side. Let's say you have $100,000. A 7% position would be 7k. You could put on 14 of those (or you could do the options replication I mentioned). Realistically speaking, you might want to start at 3% and scale up based on your conviction level. You may put on 15 5% positions and leave 25% cash (or—I'm telling you, use some of that cash to buy puts against the market or sector ETFs). This is all rule-of-thumb. Maybe you have 30 or 40 ideas that are all potential 5 baggers. You might put all of them on average size 2-3%.

It all goes back to 1) your conviction, developed using tools I introduced to you in the first 11 chapters, and 2) your mental well-being—can you sleep with the volatility a concentrated portfolio will inevitably produce? If you have done your work, and you don't need the money tomorrow or next week (AND YOU SHOULD NOT BE INVOLVED IN EQUITIES IF YOU NEED THE MONEY TOMORROW OR NEXT WEEK), then you should be fine.

Iterate, Iterate, and Iterate again

Remember the concept, "Plan, Organize, Staff, Direct, Control"? This is a feedback system; you've planned and organized the portfolio of businesses, and you staffed the project (with yourself and maybe with Me—brian@broadwaycap.com). You are now directing and controlling the process. And that's all iterative. As you move along, with your daily journal and checklists (which you now have) and you continue your scuttlebutt and review of the company's financials, your opinion of valuation may, and almost certainly will change. The market will whip around, too, so you'll need to determine if you need to resize positions (add, subtract, do nothing, use options).

I'm available to discuss all of the above.

CHAPTER 14
CONCLUSION

At this point, you are at a point where you have the basic toolkit and framework to look at, value, and buy equities and the mental gut check that should enable you to look at actually DOING it.

Maybe you don't want to spend all the time on it. That's fine. Let's talk—I can point you in the right direction, even if that means helping you buy a low-cost, highly diversified index fund. I want you to win—you already ARE a winner, so I also want to protect you from losing. You've come with me for nearly 200 pages. At this point, there are 1000s more pages for you to review, and if you don't have the time or the desire to be a learning machine, building portfolios the way I do it, let's do it together.

If you DO attempt to do it yourself, know that you're not alone and that you can—and certainly will-make mistakes, but that's an inevitable part of the process. Sizing your portfolio so you don't permanently impair your financial situation is important. Know what you can lose, and then go out and work with that in mind.

I hope that this book has given you the toolkit not only to do it yourself but also to ask the right questions when someone is being considered to do it FOR YOU. This is a lot less mystical than it sounds, and I hope you took that away.

Again, I'm available at brian@broadwaycap.com and welcome the chance to chat with you.

For further reading, please contact me on brian@broadwaycap.com or go to www.convexityhunter.com.

Made in the USA
Monee, IL
03 November 2026

67383432R00095